T0408097

LETHAL

LETHAL

340 GOALS
...in One Season

The Extraordinary Life of **PAUL MOULDEN**

Foreword by Paul Lake

First published by Pitch Publishing, 2022

Pitch Publishing
9 Donnington Park,
85 Birdham Road,
Chichester,
West Sussex,
PO20 7AJ
www.pitchpublishing.co.uk
info@pitchpublishing.co.uk

A CIP catalogue record is available for this book
from the British Library.

ISBN 978 1 80150 176 7

Typesetting and origination by Pitch Publishing

Printed and bound in Great Britain by TJ Books, Padstow

Contents

I'd like to dedicate this book to my grandad Joe and my dad Tony for giving me such sound advice and for their complete faith in me. Also, to my mum for doing whatever was needed, whenever it was needed.

Acknowledgements

I'D LIKE to thank my team-mates from Bolton Lads Club, Jimmy Hill and Billy Howarth.

At Manchester City, I'd like to thank Tony Book, Ken Barnes, Glyn Pardoe and Roy Bailey – and the scout who took me to the club, Eric Mullender.

For belief in me with England, thanks to Charles Hughes – a visionary who was dismissed by many at the time, but whose methods are widely used today.

Also, Craig Simmons and Colin Murphy at the FA for all the help and support when I needed it.

For my numerous recoveries/operations and rehab, Tony Banks and Mandy Johnson, you are in a league of your own.

The late Terry Cooper and Trevor Morgan plus the irrepressible Mr Brent Peters.

To the late Robbie Brightwell, and of course his son Ian.

A big thanks to my former team-mates Julian Darby, Paul Lake. Jason and Darren Beckford and dozens of others, too many to mention.

To Jane Camillin at Pitch Publishing for believing my story may be of interest and to everyone else who played a part in getting me back on the pitch – it meant everything to me.

Sincere thanks to you all.

Introduction

I LOVED scoring goals.

Ask any kid who loves football and, of course, they would say the same thing. Everyone loves scoring goals, right?

For me, finishing came easily and naturally, though that doesn't mean I didn't work hard at it. I wanted to be a professional footballer and, though Bolton Wanderers were on my doorstep, I wanted to play for Manchester City one day, like my hero Peter Barnes.

At Bolton Lads Club, I would literally score for fun, but at the time it didn't feel like anything special. I managed 118 goals in 1979/80, then 145 the season after, which led to a place in the *Guinness Book of Records*.

But that turned out to be what you might call the warm-up. In 1981/82, I scored 289 goals in 40 matches for Bolton Lads – 340 in all competitions – breaking my own world record and earning a second entry in the *Guinness Book of Records*.

In three years, I'd scored 603 goals in roughly 140 games and though that still has people scratching their heads, even now it just seems like something that was pretty normal and not that much to get excited about – it was always other people who made a fuss about it (except my dad and grandad!).

What I didn't realise was what a millstone around my neck being a world record holder would be.

Paul Moulden

Bolton, May 2022

Foreword by Paul Lake

THE FIRST time I became aware of Paul Moulden was when I was with a junior side called Blue Star and we were playing Bolton Lads. Before we kicked off, I became aware of what looked like a man among boys because he was broad-shouldered, powerful and he might have even had a hairy chest at that time!

I was thinking, 'Who is this guy?' – and, of course, it was Mouldy, who, I might add, was unplayable on that particular day. I think we got beat 5-4 and he scored all five of Bolton Lads' goals. After that, I felt I would remember his name without too much trouble because we had a good side and they had some decent players, but he'd been the difference between the two teams.

It had been a fascinating introduction to Paul Moulden and what he was capable of. Before too long, I heard that he had been taken on Manchester City's books and his world-record goalscoring feats became a regular topic of conversation around the age group we were at that time. I didn't know him that well, but as soon as I was picked up by City, I got to know him much better.

He was a year up from me and we played a few City A games together, but what I first noticed about Mouldy was what a caring and friendly guy he was. He made himself known, shook my hand and checked everything was OK and made it clear that he was always on hand if I ever needed advice of any kind. He made me feel welcome and at ease and he was very mindful that, as first-year YTS, I was entering the lion's den because he'd been there and knew what it felt like.

I liked him straight away.

From the moment I met him, I'd say he was the most professional footballer I ever worked with. He was meticulous in terms of his warm-ups or whatever he did. Every session mattered to Paul and there was no such thing as an 'I can't be bothered today' day. His attitude was exemplary and he was absolutely bang on it each and every time. The knock-on effect of that was that he raised the standards of everybody else, and that's quite something for a 17-year-old lad to do.

Mouldy was balancing between the A team and City's reserve side and it wasn't that long before myself and Andy Hinchcliffe were doing the same thing as well. But because he was so powerful, he was an unbelievable threat in and around the box. Left foot, right foot, he could make the ball move all over the place and he hit at different angles to make it do weird and wonderful things. His movement and anticipation were on another level and it was clear that this was the main reason he scored so many goals. His instinct as a young player was magnificent, and that's not something I say lightly.

He worked so hard on his technique and how he used his body to get in front of people and roll centre-halves. Even at 17, he wasn't only physically stronger, intellectually he was a very clever footballer who was almost beyond his years.

I played alongside him up front quite a few times, but it was more as a provider who made a few goals for him rather than anything else. I scored one or two, but his movement made it so easy for me and once he was within sight of goal, he just pounced on things. He was electric, and in and around the 18-yard box, he came to life.

As we got older, and physically some of the other boys got bigger and stronger themselves, he wasn't able to leave people in his wake as he had once done but get him in the 18-yard box and it didn't matter what size they were. Case in point, the FA Youth Cup semi-final against Arsenal. They were favourites to win the game and were 2-0 up, but Mouldy scored twice in five minutes – goals only he could have scored – and it was those moments when he dropped a shoulder and got a shot away when often he had no right to.

Of course, we went on to beat Manchester United in the final that year and win the FA Youth Cup for the first time, but I'm certain we wouldn't have won it without Mouldy.

He was a player we looked up to because if we were struggling and trying to make something happen, you always looked to Mouldy, and when he was on it we knew we were going to be all right – and this was a team that included Steve Redmond, Ian Brightwell, Ian Scott and David White and many other talented lads.

It wasn't long before he was in and around the first team, but he was competing against the likes of Imre Varadi, Wayne Biggins and Trevor Morley – players who had been brought in by the club and had more experience – plus Darren Beckford who had come through the ranks, and he was never given the run of games he needed to settle into the side and do what he did. It was a regular frustration for him, but as good as the strikers he was up against for a first-team berth, you have to ask were any of them better than Mouldy? With respect to all of the guys mentioned above, the answer is no.

It was all down to Mel Machin's interpretation of what Mouldy could offer and he just opted for experience up front. Mouldy did play for the first team a few times and he did score goals because it was in his DNA. Had he been given time and assurances that he was going to get a good run, he would have delivered. He was lethal and he would have scored over and over again.

But Imre Varadi was in the box seat and scoring because he'd been given a run of games to do that, so it will always be a case of 'what if?' – what if Mouldy had been given a run of 20 or 30 games? What could he have achieved? Unfortunately, we will never know but it's a question I'd always be asking if I were in Paul's shoes.

Mouldy's attitude was always spot on and, yes, he had more than his fair share of major injuries, but credit to the man because he always came back. I believe that if Machin had trusted him more, he would have got the best out of Mouldy who would have brought the best out of other people, but as time went on, Paul's frustrations began to show towards the manager and that is completely understandable.

We always had his back and looked out for him, and we used to joke that Tony Book ('Skip') used to absolutely love Mouldy. The one thing you'd always hear Skip say during games he was playing in was, 'Paul Moulden! Paul Moulden! Well done, son!'

All the lads who played alongside Mouldy hold him in the highest regard because he was an unbelievable footballer. A top player, a top professional and the question will always be – and it's the one I wonder about my own career – what might he have achieved if he'd stayed fit?

But despite all that, I never once heard him complain about the wretched luck he had and never let it be said that

Paul Moulden was anything other than one of the best young players in English football at that time.

I am proud to call him a friend of mine.

Paul Lake

Manchester, May 2022

1

The Apprentice

MY FIRST appearance of any kind was on 6 September 1967, when I entered the world – probably screaming, but undoubtedly kicking! – as Paul Anthony Joseph Moulden (my middle names after my grandad Joe and dad Tony). I was the youngest of two children my parents would have, my sister Helen having arrived 18 months earlier.

We didn't have much as a family – in financial terms – but we had more than enough to live a fairly humble and happy enough existence, if that makes sense.

We lived in Tonge Fold, a small village about a mile outside the town centre in Bolton. It has the A57 dissecting it and two rivers – the River Tonge and Bradshaw Brook – either side of what was a pretty close-knit community. My grandad Joe lived around the corner, but I never met my grandma, who had died young, leaving him a widower.

I would spend a lot of my time with my grandad growing up, but that wasn't because of childcare issues, as my mum didn't work – it was just down to the fact that I thought the world of him and loved being in his company.

The first memories I have of football are from watching my dad playing semi-pro at a decent level and of me kicking a ball around in front of my grandad's house. My dad was a winger who was about to become an apprentice with Blackburn Rovers, but my grandad, who had let him do all the schoolboy standard football up to that point, told him he needed to get a trade under his belt first.

Joe had been a Japanese prisoner of war and was a roofer back on civvy street, and he insisted my dad needed something he could turn to other than football in case things didn't turn out. Plus, my great aunt said my dad needed an education, too, so they were both worldly-wise and could spot the potential pitfalls of a life in football, which wasn't particularly well paid back then.

So, his apprenticeship at Blackburn became an apprenticeship in a local garage and he actually ended up with no club at all for a time as a result. But it wasn't long before Bury found out he was unattached and offered him the chance to play part-time, with training on Tuesdays and Thursdays, which he accepted. That meant he had games on Saturdays for the Bury A and B teams plus the odd reserve match here and there. He did well and eventually progressed to the first team and within a few months, he'd played well enough to win a transfer to Peterborough United, who were the up-and-coming team in the Fourth Division at the time with big ambition and a bit of money behind them. On his debut, he played alongside nine internationals, so it was a decent club with a great squad.

By the time I was born, Dad had moved into non-league football and when I was old enough, my grandad took me along to watch him. It was a football-mad household and if you weren't a player, you weren't allowed in. There were footballs all over the house and I fell in love with the game almost as soon as I could walk. I'd be out on the field near our house or on Hind Street where my grandad lived – he'd always lived there and never moved from his humble two-up, two-down terraced house.

In fact, nearby Leverhulme Park was somewhere I spent much of my younger life, whether it was cross-country running, or playing football with mates, my grandad or whatever.

My first experience of organised football was when I was selected for my primary school team at St Osmond's, aged nine. I was only slightly built but could run forever so the coach put me up front. There was a slight issue, though – the actual rules of the game were a mystery to me, and I had no idea about offside, so I was all over the shop and continually getting caught out. I had all the parents shouting at me from the sidelines, so that night, my dad sat me down and explained it all to me. He got out the Subbuteo pitch and put players in positions and by the time he'd finished, the penny had dropped, and I never looked back.

I hadn't been to watch any games up to that point, but my grandad took me to see Bolton Wanderers versus Everton at Burnden Park on Boxing Day 1976 and we sat in the Main Stand, but neither club were destined to be 'my team'. I have my aunt to thank for that!

After her mum died (she was my dad's sister, for the record), she went away to be a nun for a while in Manchester and I remember she came home one Christmas with a Manchester City shirt with the Umbro diamonds down each arm, just like my hero Peter Barnes. I loved it and my dad suggested I buy the shorts and socks to go with it from the money I'd been given from other people. So, we got on the train and, if memory serves, got off in Darwen and then walked all the way to Maine Road! It was a hell of a hike, and we approached the stadium from behind the Kippax and walked around the front and it was like, 'Jesus Christ! This is Manchester City's ground. Wow!' It was unbelievable.

We went into the souvenir shop, and I was literally like a kid in a sweet shop, just in awe of it all, and I found the shorts and socks in my size, bought them and that was that – I was a Blue for life. I remember Gerald Sinstadt was doing a six-week feature on City for *Granada Reports* (I think) and on Peter Barnes in particular and I'd watch each episode in my full City kit aged ten, dreaming of one day playing like him. He was class and I always remember him playing for England against Brazil and I thought he looked like he should have been playing for Brazil rather than England.

For me, it was football morning, noon and night and I had a thirst to get better and improve as much as I could, practising, practising, practising. I was lucky to have my grandad as a mentor because he was so forward-thinking and, in many respects, way ahead of his time. As an example, my sister was an academic high achiever, but she used to get nervous around exam times and when she took her 11-plus to apply for a grammar school, she failed because her nerves got the better of her. My grandad told my dad that the only place for Helen was a grammar school where they would educationally challenge her, and so he insisted my dad find another way to get her in. So, he applied for a scholarship for her – which she was awarded – and today Helen is headmistress of a local primary school.

My dad knew that round pegs went in round holes and in me, he'd seen a spark of something, and he nurtured that in a simple but effective way. He set about helping me improve my game by being the best I could be at the basics. He could see that from my early matches, I was very much right-footed and he knew that in order to have any chance of making it – or at least being as versatile as I could be – I needed to be able to use both feet when playing (rather than using my left just to stand on!). We had three Casey footballs – the heavy leather ones with the laces across the top that were like a rock when they were wet – all size fours, which was one down from the ones adults used.

So, every night in the summer, we used to go on to the field opposite my grandad's house. He made me wear a black galosh on my good foot and my boot on my left. He knew that when it came to shooting practice, if I tried to hit a Casey with my galosh on (which was a bit like a black PE plimsole), I'd likely break my foot! As a result, I'd only shoot with my left and, gradually, I got better and better and it started to show in games, too.

I just loved scoring goals, as most kids do, but it became my passion because, though I practised my all-round game regularly, maybe 90 per cent was focused on my finishing and I quickly learned that if you could score goals, you had currency at school and, in some ways, general life. It made you popular among your peers and also among older kids and I, like all kids, wanted to be liked.

I remember taking part in games at Leverhulme Park with lads who were three, four or even five years older than I was and more than holding my own. One day, my dad wandered over to watch me and when he saw the size of some of them (I was being marked by a couple of six-footers with beards!) he pulled me out and told me that if I ended up with a broken leg, it would only be me who lost out. I was raw, but already decent in front of goal and could stick it away when I got the chance. He was right, of course, but it was actually a great grounding for me as time moved on.

Saturday mornings had always been about lying in bed and watching *The Banana Splits* and *Here Come the Double Deckers* on TV, while outside I could hear the sound of football boots on concrete, walking across the playground to the pitches in the secondary school near our house. But now, as I progressed, I was one of those lads walking across, making that noise with my studs and it was all just magical and exciting.

Now offside-savvy, I remember a game against Church Road where I scored both goals in a 2-2 draw – they are sort of my first 'official' goals that I can recall. They were a big rival at primary school level and afterwards, my team-mates and the parents were like, 'Wow, you scored two goals against Church Road!' and it clearly meant something, but for me, they could have been Manchester United or Rochdale – I didn't have a clue if scoring against them was different from anyone else. But to others, it was pretty special and that stuck in my head. What I was aware of was that feeling of elation when I saw the ball hit the back of the net. It was like an adrenaline rush that surged through my body – I've never taken drugs in my life, but I imagine that's the feeling users are chasing all the time. An instant and addictive high.

That was in my last year at primary school. Academically, I was struggling a bit, but in all honesty that was mainly because I just wasn't interested. I remember my mum being called in to see the headmaster who told her that my reading and writing was substandard for my age.

I was always in the remedial groups, but what nobody had worked out was why my ability to concentrate was nil and why I was so easily distracted. My auntie Madeleine was a lecturer, and she clocked the problem straight away. She asked me where I sat when I did the remedial work and if, by any chance, it was in the canteen with the large glass windows. I said it was and she asked me which way I faced, and I told her that I always sat facing the window so I could see what was going on outside

She looked at my dad and said, 'That's why he's not bothered, Tony!'

My mum asked if I could bring my army books and comics in to read because of the enthusiasm I had for them at home, where I'd get a regular supply from my cousin. I wasn't interested in the pirate and mystery island books they had in school, but anything to do with soldiers or westerns and I was all over it. If there was a John Wayne film on, I'd race home from wherever or whatever I was doing to make sure I didn't miss it. My mum would shout me in and my bath would be run, then it was dinner, pyjamas and a war movie or western. It was brilliant.

The school weren't interested in letting me bring my own stuff in to read and so things carried on the way they had been. I suppose they couldn't really accommodate that, or all the kids would be asking why they couldn't read the *Beano* and *Dandy* instead of doing maths!

At Christmas, we had a school day trip to a circus in Blackpool and when I got back, I was full of this and that, brimming with enthusiasm and my aunt asked me if I'd enjoyed it. I told her it was the best thing I'd ever seen, and she just shook her head and said, 'Why are they taking *you* to the circus? You should be the only one still in class because you're not doing your work.'

And she was right, but she was also the only one who could see what was really happening, so as regards learning, I could tell you what was going on and what was happening in school but only because I watched it from the remedial table! Schoolwork? It was the last thing on my mind.

I'd progressed enough by now to play for the Bolton Boys Federation under-12s and was doing well. Whenever I used to go and watch my dad play after school with my grandad, the older guys who spoke to him asked how I was doing and would always say, 'Can he play a year young?' I didn't understand what they meant, but Joe would always say, 'Aye, he can hold his own.' What they meant was, could I play up a year or two in organised games?

I was doing OK, scoring goals for my team and learning all the time. But everything was about to get put on hold as I had my first real setback.

It came playing for Bolton Boys during a game for the under-12s at ten years old and I suffered what would be my first leg break. It was on Worsley Common, and I was going through on goal when I just got cleaned out by this lad who came from nowhere. Looking back, it would be the first of many similar challenges I was on the end of. Parents watching later said it was one of the worst tackles they'd ever seen, but to me, I was just clattered, and I hadn't seen it coming. I crumpled down on the grass straight after in agony.

Our coach Len ran on. He had this can of 'magic spray' which he proceeded to empty on my injured leg, which was now almost black because I'd snapped my tibia and fibula straight through. As serious as it was at the time, I still piss myself laughing when I look back and remember how Len was quite pleased with himself, saying, 'Bloody hell, it's good stuff this innit?' He thought the spray was bringing the bruising out, so I said, 'Yeah, Len, magic – but it still really hurts.'

Eventually, I was helped off and taken straight to Bolton Royal Infirmary where the X-rays showed both bones had been broken clean through and poor Len couldn't stop apologising, probably because he'd believed I would be able to carry on playing if he put enough of his miracle spray on! It still cracks me up even now. But at the time, after I got back from hospital with my full leg in plaster, reality kicked in that I wouldn't play football again for at least 16 weeks – and that feels like a lifetime for any ten-year-old.

It was the first broken bone I'd ever had, but if there was one thing that made it easier, it was that my team didn't play for around 12 weeks while I was out because continuous heavy rain had waterlogged all the pitches, and that was followed by a long period of freezing weather meaning the sodden pitches had become rock hard and unplayable. My dad told me to be patient and that the games would still be there for me by the time I recovered.

I remember when I finally got my leg out of plaster, I went down to watch the lads train on a Tuesday evening, and I was itching to get back out there with them. On the Saturday, I went down again to training and said I'd go in goals for a bit, just to be involved. Within a few minutes of the session starting, I raced out to clear the ball and collided shin-to-shin with another lad and immediately felt agonising pain.

It was straight back to hospital where it was touch and go whether they put the plaster cast back on because they were worried that one more knock on my shin and I'd be in big trouble. They didn't do anything in the end other than remind me of the consequences, but it was a warning for me, and my dad told me I wasn't to start playing again properly until everything was bang on.

So I waited about another eight weeks until my ankle felt free and my leg was strong again. My dad had given me an exercise regime to strengthen the muscles during the interim which worked as well as any physio plan or advice I'd been given. All in all, I'd had about six months out and towards the end, I was desperate to get back and start scoring goals again.

That's what I lived for.

2
Unlucky Break

I WAS lucky that my secondary school, Thornleigh Salesian College, turned out to be very sporty. They were high achievers in sport as well as education, but if you were good at one but not the other, that was fine, too – that suited me down to the ground. It had been a top grammar school for many years but we were in the first year of Margaret Thatcher's initiative to turn grammar schools into comprehensive schools, so all of a sudden this prestigious independent college had a bunch of numbnuts like me wandering around!

They didn't know what had hit them. I lived in the catchment area for Thornleigh, and they were now stuck with me and a load of other kids who wouldn't have got anywhere near their induction criteria before Maggie's shake-up.

Let's just say it was an education of convenience in that whenever the chance for me and others like me to be out of school arose, on some sporting activity or excursion, it was always encouraged over schoolwork. That said, I was actually representing Thornleigh really well in a sporting sense, and in any inter-school competitions, I never once got beat at cross-country or 1500m and I even ran for Bolton Harriers on and off for a while. All except for just one summer when I lost a race in Crewe on a sunny afternoon a few years later. This blond-haired lad who ran like a pro and looked like he had swallowed ten packs of Duracell batteries glided across the finish line ahead of me and I thought, 'Who the hell is that?' Turns out it was Ian Brightwell, my future team-mate at City – who also happened to be the son of Olympians Robbie Brightwell and Ann Packer!

I was county standard, but cross-country always fell at the same time as football on a Saturday morning so there was only ever going to be one winner there.

My home life was football and spending as much time as possible with grandad. My dad and mum were always there for me and we didn't want for anything that we really needed, but my dad worked and he was out playing a lot of the time – plus he was being paid for the games he played, so the extra money came in handy. I had such a close bond to my grandad, it all just worked well for us as a family.

One time, a local club in Bolton were involved in a tournament up in Glasgow and I was invited to play, so grandad travelled up to Scotland with me and they were handing out these fish-paste sandwiches on the coach on the journey back. My grandad said, 'I'm not eating that and don't you bother, either – we'll get some chips in a bit.' I was starving and it took about four hours before we got off and got some fish and chips in Bolton. It's funny how things like that stick in your mind but I remember that day vividly.

I have a load of random memories about my younger years and they almost all revolve around football, like the time I left my boots at school after a Saturday morning game there. It was always my school team in the morning and Bolton Lads in the afternoon. My dad said not to worry, and that we'd go back and get the caretaker to let us in, but he had gone by the time we arrived. There was only one thing for it – we had to go to Woolworths and buy a new pair of boots; it doesn't take a genius to figure out a department store wasn't the best place for an up-and-coming footballer to buy footwear. They were cheap, plastic and nasty, but I had to play in them, and against lads who were a couple of years older than me, but I held my own.

Once my leg mended properly, my focus was solely on Bolton Lads Club under-12s. Things really started to happen and the next four years would be pretty special and end up with me going into the *Guinness Book of Records* – and as I mentioned previously, what a millstone around my neck that would turn out to be in years to come.

3
Goals, Goals, Goals

IN 1979/80, Bolton Lads were unstoppable. I didn't manage to score against Farnworth Boys in our first game that season, but I did find the net 19 times in our first five games. I ended up scoring 27 hat-tricks (many double hat-tricks and a few triple trebles) and by the time I reached 99 goals, I was like a nervous cricketer waiting to grab the single that would secure a century. Did it get inside my head? You bet. I went three games without scoring (a proper goal drought!) before I managed to get my 100th and would go on to score a total of 124 goals that season.

It was our first year together as a team; that same group of lads would stay together for the next five years and cause carnage for defences around the north-west in the process. Jimmy Hill – not *the* Jimmy Hill from *Match of the Day* – was our coach, along with my dad and Billy Howarth, who also had a son in the team.

The local paper had started taking an interest in me for some reason, with stories of my goals taking up quite a few column inches at the time. It was around then that my mum and sister started cutting them out and pasting them into a scrapbook, along with some of my own typed summaries of the games I was playing in.

I've always maintained these stats have been of more interest to others than to me, but when discussing writing this book, it became clear that some people wanted to know more about it. I've never been a 'look what I did' kind of person, but if I'm going to break everything down, I suppose this is the place to do it.

My scrapbook and news clippings have my season as this for Bolton Lads under-12s (1979/80):

Farnworth Boys: 6-1, 0 goals
Bury Hotshots: 5-1, 2 goals
Rose Lea: 11-0, 8 goals
St Peter's: 14-0, 4 goals
Marauders: 11-0, 5 goals
Smithills: 5-0, 4 goals
Unsworths: 1-1, 0 goals
Brenshaws: 18-0, 2 goals
All Saints: 8-0, 6 goals
Atherton Red Rose: 13-0, 3 goals

Christ Church: 12-0, 3 goals
Moss Bank: 5-1, 1 goal
Smithills: 6-0, 3 goals
Bury Hotshots: 11-0, 5 goals
Rose Lea: 18-1, 7 goals
Marauders: 9-0, 3 goals
Marauders: 2-1, 1 goal
St Peter's: 9-0, 5 goals
Brenshaws: 10-0, 4 goals
Unsworths: 9-0, 5 goals
High Lawn: 9-0, 6 goals
All Saints: 6-1, 3 goals
All Saints: 6-0, 1 goal
Farnworth: 7-0, 4 goals
Smithills: 6-1, 4 goals
High Lawn: 15-0, 9 goals

We won the league in a canter that season, plus the Jubilee Cup. But, as we'd been playing in a league where we were actually all a year younger than our opponents, it wasn't as easy as it might look on paper – despite some of those scorelines – so the coaches decided we should play the following season against our own age groups instead.

We played our games at Hacken Lane, and Bolton Lads were the best club you could play for in town, or probably within a 100 miles with indoor facilities and their own grass pitches. It was a well-run outfit, and I wouldn't have dreamed about playing anywhere else back then.

The following season, when I turned 13, we were playing in the under-14s league and the goals kept going in. Everything seemed to click. We were fitter than most teams and a lot stronger, plus we had better players. My main job was to hold the ball up when it was played to me and there was never any pressure on me scoring goals – but I put pressure on myself to find the net as often as I could. The moment the ball was at my feet, and I was in range, I would be looking to score. It was instinctive and predatory. I was a finisher and if I scored one, I'd want another and another. I can't speak for every striker in the world – maybe everyone feels like that – but that was what made me tick on a football pitch.

I was taking free kicks, corners, penalties – anything that gave me a chance of scoring and I bagged another 157 in total that year, making it a total of 282 in my first two seasons at the correct age level.

My goals record for Bolton Lads Club B in 1980/81:

Venue	*Score*	*Opponents*	*My goals*
H	23-0	Daisy Hill	10
H	10-1	Christ Church	7
A	7-1	Marauders	5

H	16-0	St John's	9
A	8-2	Atherton	4
A	7-3	Smithills	3
A	9-0	St Bernadette's	7
H	15-0	Bridgewater	8
H	8-2	Lads Club C	4
A	9-2	St Peter's	8
H	17-4	St Peter's	8
H	7-4	Unsworths	2
H	8-1	St Bernadette's	5
A	9-1	St John's	5
A	10-0	Daisy Hill	6
A	3-1	Unsworths (cup)	2
H	8-1	Marauders (cup)	6
A	20-0	St Williams	12
H	6-2	Rose Lea	4
H	4-1	Lads Club C (cup)	3
A	4-0	Bridgewater	3
H	9-2	Atherton	4
H	25-0	St Williams	14
A	6-0	Unsworths	3
H	5-4	Smithills	1
A	5-4	Lads Club C	3
A	6-1	Christ Church	3
H	6-1	Marauders	3

N	3-3	Smithills (cup final)	2
N replay	4-3	Smithills (cup final)	3
Games played: 30		Total goals: 157	

It had been a decent season! We won the Bolton Federation and the Lancashire FA Youth Cup.

What I didn't know was my grandad's stepbrother, Billy Horrocks – a staunch Labour man who was always writing letters to the *Bolton Evening News*, airing his political views on this and that – took it upon himself to research and, if need be, verify that my goalscoring that year was actually some sort of record. That meant collating all the information, getting the opposition coaches to sign it, getting referees to confirm details and then the league needed to sign it all off as accurate. It was a massive undertaking for him, but there were 11 goals I scored in the Lancashire FA matches that couldn't be verified, so I'd actually scored 168, but Billy managed to get all the others officially recognised and sent it off to the *Guinness Book of Records* to see if I had broken any records.

It turned out I had – the previous high was 111 by William Wright of Suffolk, so after they checked the documentation and confirmed its authenticity, that was that. My 157 goals in one season were officially a world-record haul for an amateur player at any age level anywhere in the world. It was published in the 1983 edition – along with my photo – but by then, I had already broken my own record as I'll explain shortly. It also stated that I'd scored 51 goals in other competitions, so the actual figure was 208 in total from around 45 games (plus the 11 unaccounted LFA goals). Did it make me arrogant, cocky or big-headed? Not at all – it was other people who thought it was special; I just loved seeing the net bulge.

Hand on heart, I can honestly say that nothing happening felt anything other than normal at the time and because of my upbringing, I was always fully grounded. My dad and grandad saw to that. The local papers treated things differently and I'd rarely be off the back pages for a couple of years by that point, with my mum and sister studiously collecting every clipping in what would become a volume of scrapbooks.

Scouts were starting to come and watch our games and I remember one match against Pegasus when I heard that Tony Book and Ken Barnes from Manchester City were there, and I could hear whispers that they'd come to watch a few of the Pegasus lads and that pissed me off no end, so I told my team-mates, without any intended arrogance, 'Yeah, right – they've come to watch us.' And they had. Stuff like that motivated me to give them a good show, no matter who we were up against. And more often than not, that was what I did.

Put it this way, if they really had come to see anybody else, I'd make sure they left thinking of Paul Moulden of Bolton Lads Club.

4

Keeping Count

IF THE 1980/81 season with Bolton Lads had been good for the team and for me, things were about to go off the charts. We'd been together for three years now and were probably as good as any team in our age group in the country.

I came into 1981/82 injury-free and as fit as a fiddle. My world record of 157 goals for last season was known in some circles, but it hadn't reached fever pitch just yet. Besides, I had broken my own record about halfway through the campaign.

There was never any pressure on me to score, but that season my dad kept his own records and so did Billy Howarth, his fellow coach. They did it independently of each other and neither knew the other was recording the stats from each game, but those records would come in very handy later on. I suppose they must have sensed something, or maybe just wanted a free copy of the *Guinness Book of Records*!

Our team played what I call proper football and my dad would be shouting on the touchline, 'Ball to feet! Ball to feet!' It was about playing the game the right way and progressing us as footballers over anything else. For this season in particular, I'll update my stats after each game.

We kicked off against All Saints at Hacken Lane, beating them 12-0 with eight coming from me. I always maintain that, yes, my finishing was good, but it was the lads around me who allowed me to score so many. Julian Darby was banging them in as well and we were just steamrollering everyone we came up against.

Played 1, goals 8

Next up, we were home to St Williams three days later. It was another home game and it was another trouncing – we never got cocky with big wins; we were just a machine from minute one to the final whistle. It must have been demoralising for the teams we were up against, but it felt like we were on a mission to just be as good as we could be and we beat teams by as many as we could. This one ended 16-0 and I managed to score 11 of them, so happy days and a fairly decent start!

Played 2, goals 19

Our third game was away to Farnworth Boys, and I can't speak for the opponents, but it was becoming a cause for celebration in itself if a team scored against us – from the opposition's view, not ours! We conceded our first goal of the season against

Farnworth, but still headed back home having hit double figures – a 12-1 win – and I'd added another eight to my seasonal tally.

Played 3, goals 27

Christ Church at home and another big win, but I was that hungry for goals that I was disappointed to only score five in a 13-0 win. Still, it kept things ticking along and we'd kept another clean sheet, so it was all good and I knew it wasn't all about me, it was about keeping our run going.

Played 4, goals 32

Game number five – all had been within the first fortnight of September 1981 – saw me manage a personal best. We were up against a team that included a lad from school, who was affectionately named 'Fat Baz'. All week he'd been telling me how his club, Sharples, had a really good team and that they were going to 'do us' this time. Baz wasn't that fat, as it was, but he was big and gobby. Actually, he was a lovely lad – he just never shut up! So much so, that I told our lads about what he'd been saying and that day, my goals did mean something to me, because although I liked Baz, we wanted to put him and his team in their place that day, and we did. We beat Sharples 28-0 at Hacken Lane and, if we were presented with a match ball for scoring a hat-trick, I'd have been taking five home that day as I scored 16 of our goals. It was an 80-minute game, so I averaged one goal exactly every five minutes that day. Sharples were a poor side, probably created by some bloke who got 15 kids together and found a pitch to play on. We wouldn't normally have been that harsh against a side of that calibre, but Baz had set his mates up by stoking our fire. 'Fat' Barry Fitzharris, please take a bow. With five games played, I was nearing my half century already.

Played 5, goals 48

A trip to Brenshaw was next, but it didn't matter who we were up against or where – it was usually the same outcome. Opposing strikers would rarely see the ball, opposing defenders never had a moment's peace and opposition goalkeepers ended with a bad back picking the ball out of the net so often. The final score in this one was Brenshaw 0 Bolton Lads 18. I added eight more to my total.

Played 6, goals 56

We ended a pretty decent September with our seventh win out of seven games, away to Moss Bank. We won 15-0 and I managed a double hat-trick.

Played 7, goals 62

Next up, Turton. Our overall record of 114 goals for and just one against must have been a nightmare for any opposing coach at that level. I'm not sure how you could stop us as we had quality all over the park from back to front, and this ended 14-0 with eight more to add to my own total.

Played 8, goals 70

Sutton were our next opponents at Hacken Lane and what was now a familiar pattern continued as we beat them 15-0, and I managed a triple hat-trick.

Played 9, goals 79

We had a break from Bolton Federation games next, taking on Marauders away in the cup. We conceded our second goal of the season in this one, but still won 14-1 with another triple hat-trick added on for me.

Played 10, goals 88

We returned to league action against St Peter's, and it was another big win – this time 18-1 – and I added another triple hat-trick. If I'd been given match balls every time, I'd have had enough to open a sports shop by now. Onwards and forwards!

Played 11, goals 97

We'd been drawn against Marauders in the Lancashire FA Cup, and they gave us a much harder game this time. Whether they'd learned lessons from the 14-1 beating two weeks before or not, I don't know, but this turned out to be the first time we'd failed to hit double figures and the 5-1 scoreline was our lowest of the season. I'd needed a hat-trick to reach 100 and managed to get one, plus one more for good luck. My 157 world record was in sight – all I had to do was stay fit and keep scoring.

Played 12, goals 101

It was back to the Bolton Fed for our next game, away to Atherton Red Rose, and the Bolton Lads machine rolled on with our second-biggest win of the season. We beat them 19-0, I scored ten and we moved on.

Played 13, goals 111

Because of my previous goalscoring feat in 1980/81, this time my great uncle was also able to verify results and gather paperwork as we went along. I was averaging 8.5 goals per game and when you're in the middle of something like that, it just feels normal. Our return league game against St Williams saw us just keep on rolling, though the fact they scored twice was a shock to the system! In the grand scheme of things, it didn't matter that much as we won 14-2 and I was able to keep my average more or less with another eight.

Played 14, goals 119

If we were having a monopoly on the Bolton Fed, it was fitting that we played Park Lane next in the Lancashire FA Cup. We beat them 11-0 – I got another eight and we moved on.

Played 15, goals 127

It was back to cup action in our next game, against Roselea. Six more goals for Moulden in a comfortable 11-0 win.

Played 16, goals 133

Another eight to the total followed in a 14-1 win over Farnworth Boys. Scoring never got boring and there was no feeling like it, time after time.

Played 17, goals 141

We were progressing well in the Lancashire FA Cup and a home tie with St Jude's would see me score all but two of our goals as we beat them 12-0. It was also good because I was about to hit my leanest part of the season.

Played 18, goals 151

We'd beaten Atherton Red Rose 19-0 earlier in the season, but Atherton Laburnum Road were a different proposition. It was our first real test of the season and an LFA Cup match that we were desperate to win because we wanted to collect as many trophies as we could. They had a great team that included Warren Aspinall, who went on to play for Aston Villa and Wigan, and a load of other good players we knew about from previous years. We needed a strong ref for games like that because they were tough, physical battles. We knew their best players and they knew ours and so both teams would target those individuals and try and kick them out of the game. On that day, they defended well and kept yours truly fairly quiet but I was always confident I'd get at least one decent chance – and I did – but that was the only goal of the game. A 1-0 win against a very good side.

Played 19, goals 152

Next up was an LFA Cup semi-final clash, this time against Pegasus. It was on Valentine's Day 1982 and Pegasus were considered to be one of Greater Manchester's elite teams, but they were so good that they couldn't get in a league, so the LFA Cup was the big one for them. They had a team that included David White, Paul Lake, Steve Redmond, Aiden Murphy and many other talented lads in their side. We'd lost against them the year before at under-13 level in the LFA Cup when we gave away 12 months, but we weren't going to let that happen in our own back yard.

My dad insisted we had linesmen for that game because he didn't want a coach from either side running the lines. We were focused and on it that day and as each of our lads arrived, you could just tell that our focus was total. I used to goon about a bit, but not that day and it is the first real memory I have of realising how focused being a footballer could be. We beat them 6-2 at Hacken Lane and I scored three of them. You could see they weren't used to getting turned over, but it proved that we weren't just turning over rubbish sides in the Bolton Fed. Yes, we were miles ahead of most teams we faced in our league, but it was because we were that good – and when we came up against teams that were really strong, we still beat them.

Played 20, goals 155

It was in this game that I moved past my own world record of 157, when we played Brenshaw at home in the league. We won 8-1, I got six and only injury could stop me setting a new one – not that it meant that much to me. It was just numbers; I just loved playing football

My dad wouldn't allow me to think what I was doing was anything special, and I was full-on, playing all the time. I never sat down and thought about it all as I always had something going on and was training or playing pretty much every day.

Played 21, goals 161

Marauders must have been sick of the sight of us. Our third win over them that season saw us hit 13 without reply at Hacken Lane. My seven goals took me past my previous best and would eventually take me into the record books again, though we were only halfway through the season by that stage. It also resulted in a story in the *Bolton Evening News,* who called me 'cricket-mad' – but they meant that my goals tally was more like a cricketer's score. Cricket and I didn't really go together. I was a big, strong lad at a school run by priests and I remember Father Conway made me play in a game once, which was the best thing ever. We were up against Chorley Grammar School and Father Conway thought I'd make a good fast bowler.

The first over was bowled by another lad and Father Conway then gave me the nod to bowl next. Only I was up against the England schoolboys cricket captain! My first ball went for six and there was plenty of banter going on. I couldn't believe it – banter at cricket? I'd know it better as sledging today, but I'd thought it was a game for posh, educated lads. My second ball went for four and then my third went for another four. Three balls and 14 runs conceded – I was shipping runs at a similar rate to scoring goals.

It looked like my career as a fast bowler had ended before it had begun, but I continued the over and my fourth ball was struck for another four, although all the lads on my team ran over to me celebrating. I hadn't a clue what was going on but, apparently, as he'd struck the ball, he'd also hit his own wicket and was out. I gave him some as he walked past and said, 'How good are you then you c***?' – and was duly sent off by the umpire! So much for sledging. Father Conway brushed it under the carpet, thankfully, and it wasn't the end of my cricket career after all.

My mum and dad came to watch me in another game, and we were playing away, 30 overs each side, so it was going to take up much of the day. The umpire was this very tall priest who had a big nose, and all his hair was greased back – he looked like a cartoon character. He was a nice guy and this lad hit a high shot and I thought, 'I can get this,' so I sprinted towards it, dived, and managed to get my fingers under the ball just before it hit the ground. The umpire said 'not out' and I was like, 'But I got my fingers under the ball!' Father Conway shouted, 'That's out! I'm a Catholic priest so don't argue with me!' and overruled the other guy. At assembly the following Monday, Father Conway claimed it was the best catch he'd ever seen. So, I was my own worst enemy, getting the England captain out and making this worldly catch! They wanted me to carry on, but my heart wasn't really in it.

I tried rugby once for school, but during a scrum some twat bit my ear and I was thinking, 'What's all that about?' I didn't play rugby again.

Played 22, goals 168

Our first silverware of the 1981/82 season. We were up against Blackpool Rangers in the LFA Cup Final, and they were a well-drilled unit. That game sticks in my mind because there was no soap in the bath afterwards. The final was at Bromwich Street where Bolton Wanderers used to train, and it was also where Pelé once trained during the 1966 World Cup with Brazil. There were about 400 people watching that day. We were playing on the top pitch, and it looked like it had cattle grazing on it the night before. They had a goalkeeper who was the dog's bollocks and he kept them in it, but I would score both goals in a 2-0 win and Bolton Lads had another trophy to add to the cabinet.

Played 23, goals 170

It was back to league action and a team I'd hit double figures against earlier in the season – Atherton Red Rose. We'd had some pretty tough games lately, but this was back to business as usual as we beat them 25-0 and I was able to add another 15 to the total. Two hundred was now clearly in my sights.

Played 24, goals 185

Farnworth Boys were next on the fixture list in the Jubilee Cup – it ended 9-0, I got six and we had another final to look forward to. Happy days.

Played 25, goals 191

Our first league game against High Lawn was the first of six successive away matches for us. It didn't make much difference where we played, and the game ended 8-0. I scored five.

Played 26, goals 196

Roselea were next up and they breached our defence twice, but the 9-2 win kept up our 100 per cent league record and I bagged another four to take my seasonal tally up to 200.

Played 27, goals 200

I had managed five against Christ Church earlier in the season and my double hat-trick in a 7-0 win ensured I went home smiling.

Played 28, goals 206

And it went on. Sharples were next, and an 11-0 away win kept the goals flowing with eight more for me. It's fair to say we had the title sewn up by this point.

Played 29, goals 214

Sutton, like most of the other sides in the Bolton Fed, couldn't live with us. They managed to avoid conceding double figures – just – as we beat them 9-0 and I scored six of them.

Played 30, goals 220

Next, it was Smithills away – it was another easy win, this time 10-0 – and I'd bag another nine in this one but was disappointed not to hit double figures. Ah, well!

Played 31, goals 229

I got nine again three days later. We won 11-0 against Turton, but again, not hitting double figures would have been a disappointment. I never got bored of scoring goals, that is something I am certain about, no matter who we were playing.

Played 32, goals 238

Smithills must have hated us with a passion as they played us for a second time in a week. This time it was 13-0 and I added another seven to my total. Stating the obvious, maybe, but we were slightly too good for the Bolton Fed!

Played 33, Goals 245

Moss Bank fared no better as we beat them 10-0. Eight more for Moulden. Next!

Played 34, goals 253

St Peter's put up a better fight on their own pitch. It was rare we didn't hit ten or more in that spell and this was only a 7-0 win. I settled for six.

Played 35, goals 259

I hit another eight against Roselea with the season coming towards its conclusion. It was the last game before the Jubilee Cup Final, so we all knew we had to impress the coaches to make sure we were playing, as anyone who was cocky or arrogant would be dropped and we wanted another medal to add to our collection.

Played 36, goals 267

The Jubilee Cup – the league cup in effect – was against Moss Bank who we had already beaten twice that season by an aggregate of 28-0.

I'd scored half that total and added another five this time in an 11-0 win.

Played 37, goals: 272

There were three games left and we had to play them all in a week due to our cup exploits throughout the season. All Saints were first and we beat them 17-0. Just the ten goals for yours truly in this one.

Played 38, goals 282

Our run of ten clean sheets was ended against High Lawn who we beat 8-2 – only a hat-trick this time.

Played 39, goals 285

We ended the season against Marauders, beating them 14-0 to end a pretty special season. We'd won the LFA Cup, Jubilee Cup and Bolton Fed under-14s league. I managed another four in this one to end a decent year with a disappointing haul.

Played 40, goals 289

So, that was that. I repeat – and have done all my life – I can't really understand why people are so interested in my stats for that season as I was just doing what I'd always done. I guess 289 in a season is a bit unusual, but if it wasn't for my dad and Billy Howarth keeping track, I would never have known how many I'd scored and forgotten about it by the time the next season started.

Another 51 in various competitions made the total 340 – all were verified and signed off by the various parties, but in the passage of time, I no longer have the stats and goals breakdown from those matches.

I'd received plenty of attention in the local press and wider media, plus scouts had been coming to see me regularly, so it had given me a platform to kick on, and of course, when all the world record stuff became known, things went a little nuts for a time.

But as always, my dad made sure I kept focused on improving my game. The most enjoyable thing about that year was the lads I was playing alongside. We were clinical, played great football and had a camaraderie that bonded us together like brothers. We didn't need fancy tracksuits, free gear or whatever to look good – we did our talking out on the pitch and for our age were professional and focused.

But, as my good mate Fat Baz found out, if you pissed us off, we still had a few gears to shift up!

5

Raising the Bar

THINGS WERE starting to accelerate rapidly for me. The publicity in the papers didn't do me any harm. The word had clearly got around and the goals just kept going in. I was by this point starting to believe I might actually have a shot at becoming a professional footballer.

I was also told around this time that, even though I didn't have the physique of a long-distance runner, if I could do the distances in the times I was doing at 14, I had a big future in athletics – but I gave that consideration for all of half a second because the sessions were on Saturday mornings.

My fitness was as good as any footballer my age in the country, and it was one of the reasons I was scoring so many goals, and I bagged a large proportion of them in the last 20 minutes or so when the opposition were tiring. To me, I had just as much energy at full time as I'd had at the kick-off, so I felt like I was actually getting stronger as they were starting to wilt. I also had a girlfriend now, Lisa, and things had just started happening for me all at once. The flipside of all the news stories and my growing reputation in north-west football was that I was starting to become something of a scalp. Did I have an ego? I think all good strikers have an element of that, but if I did have an ego, it was only on the football pitch, certainly not off it. But it was becoming more of a story if I didn't score and a defender with any ambition knew that if they could stop me or Julian Darby scoring in a game, it made them look like a decent prospect. All of this led to me being targeted in games for, let's just say, some 'enthusiastic tackling'. But I was now a good size for my age, quick, and I had learned to look out for anyone looking to send me off on a stretcher. I could handle myself and I could give it out as well as take it. My early years of park knockabouts with older kids had served me well, and I was used to coming off black and blue.

And it turned out I was being noticed outside of Bolton as well.

In November 1980 I was selected for the North West of England v West Midlands, with the game held at Port Vale's Vale Park. I must have done well because I was then invited to Lilleshall to train with the England Schoolboys under-15s early on in the season, but there was heavy snow so it was cancelled and I came home. I was back there for a week in the summer, where I met Tony Adams, Michael Thomas and Darren Beckford there amongst others.

If I was attracting interest from professional clubs, it was largely kept away from me and wasn't something that was talked about at home. I couldn't sign for anyone until I was 15, but I was invited to start training with lads a couple of years older than me at Blackburn Rovers. It was proper hard going, but they were the first club who had actually made the effort to get me on board in some form.

Not long after that, I began training with my hometown club Bolton Wanderers under a guy called Jimmy Conway who I really liked. I enjoyed the training because he was a smashing coach and really likeable guy, and had he stayed with Wanderers, I'd have signed for them without a shadow of a doubt. But Jimmy ended up being treated badly by the club, who blamed him for bringing in several players who infringed the FA's rules and he was moved on as a result. That, in turn, made my mind up. I thought if they could treat a guy like Jimmy badly, I didn't want to be associated with them anymore – why would I want to be part of that? It was the first football decision I made myself and it was absolutely the right one.

The phone continued to ring and, next, I tried Leeds United. My dad had played with Tony Collins who was now chief scout at Elland Road, so we crossed the Pennines and I stayed with the club during the summer on a week's residential. A lot of the lads I trained with ended up going pro and they probably had the most prestigious youth-team set-up at the time and there were players like John Sheridan who had been let go by Manchester City. I did like it at Leeds, but again, it wasn't quite right for me.

Around that time, I had a season playing for a parish football team under Father Coulter, a Catholic priest who ran the team and, like a lot of catholic priests back then, he also knew Sir Matt Busby. I'd play Sunday afternoons in the Catholic League in Bolton, and we won the league the year I played for them. There wasn't a big presentation of medals or anything, but Father Coulter said he had somebody he wanted me to meet at his house, so when I went around, there was Sir Matt, who I chatted to and, as a result, I was invited to train with Manchester United – but I absolutely hated it!

Dave Sexton was the manager at the time and Norman Whiteside was at the club, a couple of years older than me and still at school. I went to a week-long residential at Kersal Moor and we'd get a lift to The Cliff each day, to go training in the morning and afternoon – but I just couldn't stomach it. Whether it was down to my allegiance to City as a kid or just the general feeling around the place, it just wasn't for me and though I was supposed to be there Monday to Friday, by Wednesday evening I phoned my dad and told him I was coming home. He said, 'But it's Manchester United,' and I just told him that I honestly didn't care and that was the end of it.

Arsenal were another top club who had come in for me and offered me a trial, but my parents weren't keen on me living in digs somewhere in London. Things were very different in the early 1980s and the cotton wool that young kids are wrapped up in these days didn't exist, plus the various safeguarding checks and suchlike just weren't there. A year or so earlier, two Bolton lads had gone to London trialling for a club and had been put in a YMCA hostel where one had been shot in the leg with an air pistol – so my mum and dad had good reason for shying away from that.

So my next destination was Everton, but as I had left United midweek, I didn't start training until Friday the same week and they were just playing five-a-side games ahead of the weekend's A team matches. I was never going to be considered for that, so it felt like a waste of time. I was about to leave after a couple of hours when one of the coaches tapped me on the shoulder and said I was needed for the staff game they always played on a Friday afternoon. I was happy enough to take part, but I remember the first-team manager Howard Kendall cleaning me out with a tackle and I ended up needing a few stitches in my shin as a result. I played on, despite the pain and blood trickling down my sock, and at the end, Kendall came up and said, 'Well done, I thought you'd go off after that. That's what we like here. Hard lads.'

I think he probably had done it on purpose to see how I'd react, so maybe I'd passed the test! I quite enjoyed the few weeks I had at Everton, but what happened next made it all insignificant, because I'd also been invited to train with Manchester City by scout Eric Mullender (who would later discover Michael Owen and Ryan Giggs) and the moment I walked into the club, I knew that it was there I wanted to be. My dad said I should go back to Everton a few more times just to make sure, but it was City that I really wanted, and my mind was made up.

I took part in a trial game at Cheadle Town, which was basically players City wanted to have a look at around my age and some of the apprentices who were already on their books, but not getting much game time. I was able to take my scoring form for Bolton Lads into that match and banged in seven, wearing the red-and-black-striped second shirt of City for the very first time. I hoped I'd made a favourable impression.

I remember my dad taking me to see Bolton Wanderers v Manchester United in the Lancashire Youth Cup around the same time, and it was a fierce game which ended up with Mark Hughes being sent off for thumping a lad. It was lively, let's just say that, but it was a chance for my dad to tell me that, while it was all well and good scoring goals for fun for Bolton Lads and winning trophy after trophy as well as training with

England Schoolboys, what we watched that day was the real thing, and the competitiveness and physicality were a couple of levels up. It was an eye-opener for me. 'This is what it's like in the big, bad world of football,' he said. As always, it was sound advice from my dad.

But I was going to have to put everything on ice for the time being – literally.

It was December 1982 and I was playing for Bolton town team against Liverpool Schoolboys at Penny Lane in Liverpool on a rock-hard, icy pitch that was unfit to play on. There was a half chance on the edge of their box, I made a dart for the ball but as I got there, their keeper came out, bounced off the ground as he dived towards my feet and hit my shin full-on. I still have the picture of me being catapulted four feet off the ground as we collided.

As I landed, I knew in an instant that I'd broken my leg again. It was the same right leg I'd broken when I was ten, but the really painful part was that I'd just received a letter from England Schoolboys to say I'd been selected from 20 into the final 16 to play for my country, and at my last training camp with England, the selectors had told me it would be between me and Michael Thomas (who would go on to have a great career with Arsenal) for the captaincy next time we played.

I'd gone into shock and was shaking but everyone thought it was because it was freezing cold anyway, but I said to my dad it was broken. He didn't think it was and we drove back to Bolton with a bag of frozen peas on it. Magic sprays and frozen peas – nature's cure for broken bones. If only! But I knew. Dad was playing himself that afternoon, so it was my mum who took me for an X-ray where a spiral fracture on my shin bone was confirmed.

I had a feeling I can only describe as, 'Fuck me. Where do I go from here?'

That was an easy answer. I'd start with another 16 weeks in a full leg plaster and no football. It pretty much wrote off the rest of the season with City and it couldn't have come at a worse time. Everything had just been clicking into place when my shin bone had snapped again. I received a really nice letter from Ralph O'Donnell, the England Schoolboys coach, saying that it was a shame that it had happened when I'd been doing so well, and he added that they would try and get me a cap at the end of the season one way or another. I got my head down, was patient and focused on picking up where I'd left off. Once again, my dad helped me plan out a physio and strengthening plan that was second to none.

It was a hard slog. I was frustrated beyond belief but because I'd been through it before, I was able to deal with it, concentrate on my return to fitness plan and be as ready as I could when the plaster came off.

6

Barry Bennell and Others

BARRY BENNELL was a well-known figure around youth football in the early 1980s. Whenever I'd seen him around, he'd have his socks rolled down around his ankles, his shorts were just pulled up too high in a way that just didn't look right, and I thought he had this cocky, overconfident attitude.

The lads who were at decent junior sides were all pretty confident because we knew we were good players and were at clubs that always did well, but he was five rungs above anybody. He was weird.

From what I heard, he was actually a good coach, but he clearly just lusted after young lads. I heard he'd always pick a different boy to give a lift home to after training. His Lotus only had two seats and it was a lure for any impressionable kid.

A ride in his car was a real draw, but on reflection, it was probably where he made his first moves to sound out whoever was with him. I personally just couldn't stand the man.

The first time my dad saw him at a training session, I'd just come out after getting a shower, and my dad was waiting in the car park as Bennell drove out in his Lotus. My dad watched him drive away and said, 'If you ever get in a car with him, you'll be opening a can of worms for yourself, son. He's a proper wrong 'un that one, stay well clear of him.' He said he'd seen Bennell watching us all and reckoned there was 'something not right with him'.

I just said, 'Ah, he's a dickhead, Dad, I don't have anything to do with him anyway.' Bennell had a massive presence about him, he looked the part, and he talked the part. He owned that flashy car and was persuasive and a master manipulator, but whatever it was he did, he managed to get away with it for years.

I wasn't a victim, and I can't get my head around why some of the lads didn't tell us what he was like as we'd have probably filled him in. He must have terrified them, and they must have felt such incredible shame and embarrassment that they would go on to hide it for years.

Dad was always a sound judge of character and one thing he always encouraged me to do was to stick up for myself. If there ever had been an occasion that Bennell had offered me a lift or whatever, I'd have told him to fuck off. That said, I never spoke to the man and he was never one of my coaches at any of the clubs I played for. Thank God.

My dad had once had an argument with another parent of a lad who went on to have a great career. Dad was arguing that Bennell was an oddball but the other parent – and he wasn't alone as others would defend Bennell – was saying my dad was wrong about him. Many years later, when it was on the news that Bennell had been extradited back to England from the USA for sex offences against young lads, that same guy called my dad and apologised; he told him he'd been right all along.

The thing was, I'm certain that kind of abuse was rife at certain amateur clubs, and I believe what happened with Bennell was far more widespread in youth football back then.

There were two lads from Bolton I recall who were both lively characters and good footballers, but thought they could get away with murder – not literally! I had many a tough game with these two lads, whether it be on Leverhulme Park or a school game; they were tough to beat. They were a year older than me, and I remember riding down Bury Road after school and passing them. They were both wearing grey tracksuit bottoms, white T-shirts and white trainers. They looked like a pair of plonkers. I was sort of laughing as I said, 'All right lads? Who's dressed you, then?'

I'd never seen a pair of white trainers in my life other than at Wimbledon where the tennis players wore Green Flash pumps!

One of them said, 'Oh, we're signing for Nova Juniors, and you get all this free stuff.' Nova Juniors, who I think changed their name several times over the years, were connected to a guy called Frank Roper who used to cut deals with major sports brands to buy their old stock in bulk. He'd sell much of it on to market traders around Manchester, but he'd also supply the stuff to the lads at the club he was associated with.

One of them went on, 'It's great. You get a free pair of boots, pair of moulded soles, two pairs of tracksuits, travelling tracksuit, training kit, and playing kit.'

I looked at them both and was thinking what a pair of stooges they looked. I just laughed and carried on my way. Those two had enough about them to deal with any dodgy stuff and I don't think anyone would have ever tried, but it illustrated how easy it was to attract young lads to various clubs.

It was later discovered that Frank Roper was a serial child abuser and paedophile, maybe one of the biggest in Manchester. I would put money on him being connected to Bennell in some way and their seedy tendrils must have spread far and wide for many years. Roper was eventually found out, but he had offences as far back as 1960 and yet he continued to be involved in young lads' football for years without any checks on his background. How was that allowed to happen?

It wasn't only different back then, it seems there was a nationwide culture of ignorance, particularly where young footballers were concerned.

At Bolton Lads, we'd just turn up in jeans and T-shirts – my jeans had been made for me by my mate Antony Burnett's dad Duncan who was a tailor, but I didn't care. In my opinion, the free gear just seemed to me like another way of luring impressionable young footballers. We still annihilated this type of team when we played them, but they looked the part if nothing else.

Roper was a tumour. I remember one of the parents telling his son to sign for Nova because it would save him a fortune, but he just said, 'No chance. I'm not going to play for them, Dad.' Rumours were rife even back then – but nothing was ever done.

Looking back further, I might well have had a lucky escape myself. When I was 12, I went away with the local inter-league team – which was a select team made from all the clubs in the league.

On a trip to the Isle of Man, I remember my dad saying, 'Now look, don't stand for any messing about.' I didn't really understand what he meant by this, and then he went on to say, 'If anyone tries to get in your bed ...'

I had no clue what he was trying to tell me so I asked him why that would happen because there was only room for me. We didn't have a phone at home at the time, and he said, 'Your mum's put your auntie and uncle's number inside your bag and a load of two pence pieces in case you need to call home. If anything at all happens, you're to call me straight away.'

I was only 12 years old and I was thinking, 'I still haven't got a clue what you're on about here, Dad!' But I didn't dare say that to him! I wondered what he was thinking. Was it a sixth sense? I've never asked him, but I trusted his instinct without question.

As always, he was on the ball. In 2022, one of the guys who had organised trips such as these was found guilty of abusing at least one boy in the 1970s and is now a convicted paedophile. He'd already committed offences but nobody bar the victim (or victims) was aware of this. Jesus. It seems now that they were everywhere back then and likely they had free rein to abuse given the opportunity. I was just lucky my dad was so switched on, but had anyone ever come anywhere near me, I'd like to think I would have made them wish they hadn't!

It was a risky time to be a teenager playing football in the north of England, as history has proved, but thank God so many of those historical abusers have finally been brought to justice.

As for those of them who are still alive and incarcerated, I hope they rot in their jail cells.

7
Off and Running

ENGLAND AND City kept in touch throughout my recovery from the broken leg I'd sustained at Penny Lane and, just as Ralph O'Donnell had said, when I was back training in April I was invited to join a 17-man England Schoolboys squad for a match at Stoke. It was exactly the lift I'd needed, though I knew it wasn't a call-up on merit at that point as such – more a really nice gesture. I wasn't fussed – I was finally realising a boyhood dream as I pulled on that England jersey for the first time. I came on with a few minutes to go to get my first cap for my country and my family and I couldn't have been prouder.

I went back, started to train with City and play for Bolton Lads a few more times and England called me up again for a training camp in Biddulph ahead of a game against Scotland at Wembley a few days later. At the first training session, O'Donnell pulled me to one side and said, 'Fucking hell,

Paul – what have you been doing? You look as good as you were before the leg break.'

I just said, 'I've been working hard, Mr O'Donnell.'

He said he could see that. I knew I had a sniff of playing a proper game for England – this time on merit – and when the team sheet went up, I was there, up front in the starting XI. I was about 90 per cent fit, but it felt fantastic and I couldn't wait to play at Wembley Stadium.

There were more than 45,000 there to watch that day, including my family, friends and my mates from Bolton Lads, which was even better. I'd had what I believed was a sympathy cap for my country, but I'd earned this one through pure determination.

It was justified, too, as I scored one goal and set another up. It was the best end to a season imaginable, given where I'd been the previous December.

Not long after my full England Schoolboys debut, my dad got a call from the FA. The guy who called was Colin Murphy and he asked Dad how I was getting on and how my leg was. Dad said he thought it had healed well and Murphy said that was good news but asked if I would go to Lilleshall to meet with one of the England physios and have some strength tests done.

So I caught the train down, met Craig Simmons, the physio, and went through various weight and stretch exercises with him. He couldn't believe I had broken my leg just six months before and asked who I'd been doing physio work with. I said, 'Nobody, I've done all the rehab myself.' He said I had one leg that was a little shorter on one side but arranged a few visits where he would tweak this or that to help me get to peak fitness. It seemed England were taking a real interest in me and it turned out it was all down to the director of coaching for the FA – Charles Hughes – who was a master tactician and thinker of the game back then.

Put it this way, if he was in the game today, he'd probably be Pep Guardiola's right-hand man. He was that good. His philosophy was that if you could win the ball back in the final third of the pitch, and have fewer than three passes forward, your chances of scoring increased by 80 per cent. So he deduced that the best way to play was to get the ball into the final third as quickly as possible – not a long-ball game, but get it forward as fast as possible and press high. If the opposition defence had the ball, it would all be about winning it back as quickly as you could, then slipping a winger or striker in and getting a shot away.

Hughes would get slaughtered for it in years to come when the national team went through some lean times, but other managers and sports journalists only took one aspect of his theory – getting it from the back to the front as fast as possible

– and beat him with it, labelling his methods as old-fashioned and basically calling him a long-ball merchant, even though he was anything but.

Hughes had taken a shine to me so I was invited during the summer to train for three or four weeks at Lilleshall, all fitness work that you were also expected to do when you went back home. There was a lot of tactical work and drills and I really bought into the Charles Hughes way, worked hard and really enjoyed it.

In fact, the first time I actually met him, he said, 'Young Moulden. Thornleigh College – that's Astley Bridge isn't it? I started my teaching career at Breightmet Grammar School; whereabouts are you based?' I told him Tonge Fold and he told me that he used to deliver sports lessons at Tonge High. 'I'll be watching you with interest, young man,' he added.

I was called up for England under-16s for a game in Reykjavík against Iceland on my 16th birthday, 6 September 1983 – not a bad way to celebrate a landmark day– and I remember a training session with Hughes beforehand when at one point he stopped the session and was telling the lads after a particular transition that if they created a similar one against Iceland, I would score.

'I'll tell you that if you give that boy a chance like that tomorrow,' he said in his educated voice, 'He. Will. Score. He'll think it's his bloody birthday!'

At that, our coach Colin Murphy chuckled to himself and Hughes looked over at him before we carried on with the session. At the evening meal later that day, Hughes called me over as I entered the dining room.

'Young Müller, come over here,' he gestured – a few of the coaches had nicknamed me after Gerd Müller, the West Germany striker, because of my finishing. 'Why didn't you say something when I mentioned it would be like your birthday when it actually is your birthday, isn't it?'

I said, 'Yes, Mr Hughes, it is. I'm 16 today.'

He produced a menu from God knows where and told me to order whatever I wanted, so I did, picking the most expensive thing I could find and went for lobster tails for two.

'Do you have many lobsters in Bolton?' he asked.

I told him no, he smiled, and he invited me to the staff table where I sat and enjoyed my lobster tea. He'd taken me under his wing and he was a pretty powerful ally to have.

We beat Iceland 2-1 the next day and I scored one of the goals. Tony Adams, John Beresford, Franz Carr, Fraser Digby, Darren and Jason Beckford and John Moncur all played in that game and I loved being away with my country.

As I was now 16, I was allowed to sign as an associate schoolboy for one of the clubs who'd shown interest in me. The good news for me was that I still had plenty to choose from, but my mind was pretty much made up and, having tried out most of the top teams around the north of England, I became an associated schoolboy with Manchester City – the only club I wanted to play for.

On the day I was due to sign schoolboy forms and make everything official, I was asked to go out on the training pitch with City manager John Bond and first-team coach John Sainty for a ten-minute skill test. I was asked to trap the ball, then turn with it to my right and then left, and Bond just said, 'Yeah, we'll sign him.'

I would be on £25 a week on a YTS plus £25 for my parents for keep until I was 17 when I would sign a three-year deal and also receive £30,000 which my dad said would buy me a house and set me up no matter how things panned out in football.

A few months later, I was invited to play for the North West of England v West Midlands again, this time at Bolton's Burnden Park, and I wasn't playing a year younger anymore as we were all the same age. It went well and I scored four goals in a 6-2 win – I had a chance to get a fifth late on and, despite the angle being difficult, I tried my luck and it hit the post and came back out. I should have scored it, I knew that, but I was greedy for goals and wanted a fifth.

I'm not sure who came to watch me from City, but when I went back to train, which was all I did for a while, Tony Book took me out on to the pitch at Maine Road with Joe

Corrigan in goal, Dennis Tueart, and a load of other first-team players. He wanted to re-enact the situation where I'd hit the post in the game at Bolton with the same angle. Booky asked the first-team players what I should have done in that situation, and they all said 'square it'. Tony shook his head and said, 'He took a shot,' then looked at me and said, 'Why did you shoot?' I shrugged my shoulders and said that we were winning 6-2, I'd already got four and thought I'd try and score another.

It was funny and the other players were laughing. But I got the message. Later in that same session, Glyn Pardoe said, 'I'm gonna show you something, Mouldy.' He asked me to try and hit the corner of the crossbar and post and, with something like my 88th attempt, I did it and Glyn went 'oooooohhhhhh!' I was thinking, 'What the hell is he up to?'

Then Glyn said, 'That's the biggest lesson you've learned this morning – you get nothing for an "oooooohhhhhh" in this game. Make sure you hit the target and get it inside of the frame of the goal.' Then he walked off. It wasn't until later on that I saw a team-mate hit the outside of the post and the crowd went 'oooooohhhhhh!' and I thought back to Glyn. He was right. You get nowt for an oooooohhhhhh. What a great lesson to have learnt from Glyn Pardoe, and on Maine Road at 16 years old. It's one I've never forgotten and that I've passed on ever since.

It was a bit unconventional at City, it wasn't black and white, and you sometimes had to fill in the picture yourself, but what Glyn explained that day would stay with me for the rest of my career.

I was settling in well and enjoyed the two sessions a week I had at Platt Lane. I'd catch the train and bus to Maine Road for the sessions on Tuesday and Thursday evenings. I'd get off at Victoria, walk to the Arndale where I'd get the bus to Princess Parkway and then cut through the houses to Platt Lane. I was happy as Larry and was loving being a City player. As a schoolboy, our existence was to make the apprentices' lives easier, laying the kit out, washing the footballs, boots, gathering kit or whatever. It was hard graft, often menial labour, but I loved it. In my first-year intake, there was Ian Brightwell, Steve Redmond, Ian Scott, David White (who everyone at schoolboy level knew could catch pigeons in a canter, he was so quick), Andy Thackery, Steve Mills and Steve Thompson. It was a great group.

My first year passed quickly – John Bond had quit in February and City were relegated on the final day of the 1982/83 season.

So, City were by now a Second Division side and Billy McNeill had taken over, with Jimmy Frizzell as his number two. In all honesty, it didn't really affect me at all as that was all at first-team level and our paths rarely crossed at that stage.

But that was about to change – at least for me. Besides, my dad believed there would be better opportunities for young players given the club's precarious financial situation and the fact several senior pros had been moved on.

It would have been around September 1983 when my dad got a call from Tony Book asking if I could possibly have the morning off school. It was arranged and Tony added that he wanted to do some running sessions. So I pitched up at Maine Road and got changed, but there were no other apprentices there and I wondered what was going on. Tony walked in so I said hello and told him I was just going to put my boots on, and he said, 'Don't worry, you won't need your boots today, son' (a saying that many young apprentices/young pros never liked to hear because you knew you were in for a hard running session!).

I was right; he told me I was going to join the first team for a running session, which was a bit out of the blue, but I thought it was brilliant as well. So, I travelled in a car with Billy McNeill and Tony Book to Chorlton Water Park where we were to do two laps of the lake, which was about a four-mile circuit. Billy told me it was a race and said, 'Go on and win it.' He'd been told about my ability to run cross-country and as we lined up ready to go, the first-team players, including Mick McCarthy, Derek Parlane, Jim Tolmie and all the rest, were all there when we set off. Nicky Reid kept up with me and though I toasted the rest, I was only just quicker than Nicky. When we got back, the gaffer went mad at the others, then asked, 'How old are you, son?' I said I was 16 and he laid into the first-teamers for being licked by a 16-year-old, though he acknowledged Nicky had at least kept up with me.

He then told us to run the route in reverse, so I set off again – the first run I'd done blind in terms of layout and distance, but now I knew the terrain and had a feel for it so I could pace myself better – and when I got back to where I'd started, Billy said, 'That was quicker than your first run!' That became a ritual for the next six weeks, with Billy saying to the rest of the lads, 'Just keep up with him.' I used to get back to school and my mates would ask where I'd been. 'Running with Man City's first team,' I'd reply, and they'd be like, 'Fuck off! No way.'

It was magical.

* * *

Tony Book's Thursday under-16s sessions at Platt Lane were superb but you needed to be fully focused throughout, and on one occasion, after a session had ended, I got into a fight with a team-mate who had taken the piss out of me. As I said earlier, we were a family who didn't have much, but we always had what we needed. So when I went into the changing rooms and found my jumper all tied up in knots, I looked around and said, 'Who the fuck's done this?' I saw Mike Milligan sniggering away and asked if he'd done it. He said, 'Yeah, well your jumper's shit anyway.'

That was it! We ended up having a proper ding-dong right there and then until Tony Book walked in, separated us, and said, 'What the bloody hell's going on here?' He reminded us we were all team-mates and I said, 'Yeah, maybe we are, but I'm not putting up with that.' Tony told Milligan he'd speak with him later.

My dad was having a coffee as he waited with the other parents. When I came out, he told me Tony had come out of the dressing rooms like a bat out of hell, so he asked me what I'd done. I told him about Milligan and the jumper and what happened, and he just told me I'd done the right thing standing up for myself.

As it turned out, Mike joined Oldham Athletic and had a long career with them and Norwich City, even spending a brief time with Everton, but we weren't finished there, were we Mr Milligan? There was that session at Oldham that went all wrong over a trip on the old AstroTurf – but that's all water under the bridge now and let's just leave it at that.

It was 6 December 1983 when I played my first proper game of any kind in Manchester City colours. My dad had received a phone call for me to be at Maine Road for 2pm as I was in the squad for an FA Youth Cup tie away to Middlesbrough. I was in my last year at school, and I was making my City debut at last, as a raw but excited 16-year-old.

In the City team that day were Darren Beckford, Ian Scott, Jason Beckford, Paul Simpson and Jamie Hoyland, while Boro had Alan Kernaghan and Peter Beagrie starting for them. I wore the number nine shirt, and it felt such a privilege to walk out in those sky-blue colours for the very first time.

It went well, too – I scored twice, played really well and we beat Middlesbrough 3-1; the perfect start. I tried to take my goalscoring instincts at schoolboy level into senior football (of sorts), so I was floating in the clouds as we travelled back to Manchester.

Training was going well, too – I was fit and sharp and I'd finally had my chance and taken it. But if a footballer's journey is occasionally helped by lucky breaks, I was about to have another break – but not the sort I was hoping for and there was nothing lucky about it either. Just 12 days after making my City debut against Middlesbrough, it happened again.

A year before, I'd broken my leg for the second time in my life while playing for Bolton Lads against Liverpool Schoolboys. Fast forward 12 months and on 19 December 1983 – almost exactly a year to the day – I broke my leg for a third time. You couldn't make it up.

It was in the Lancashire League where there was a mix of top youth teams, lower-league reserve sides and even some non-league second teams. City, United, Liverpool and Everton were all in there, plus sides such as Marine, South Liverpool, Chorley, Alsager and UMIST. It was a rare old mix of upcoming talent and gnarly old pros or players who were either not getting a look in for the first team or building their fitness up after being out injured. Often it was a case of 'put your pads on, take your bazooka, machine gun' and anything else you had to protect yourself in these brutal games.

After my FA Youth Cup debut away to Middlesbrough, I played for City's A team (as it was called) at home to Stockport County in the Lancashire League. I remember running out and seeing what I thought was the comedian Bob Carolgees, who used to be famous for having Spit the Dog on his arm. It turned out to be Micky Quinn but when I first clocked him, I thought, 'That's him off TV!' He must have got that all the time back then.

It was a Saturday morning, and my dad came along and watched and said that I'd held my own in that game. Given that I was still at school, I was really pleased with that, but it was an eye-opener because we were up against grown, experienced blokes and the physical side of it was demanding to say the least.

The next week, we were away to Chorley and my dad, who had played enough semi-pro football to know what he was on about, warned me before the game, 'Watch yourself today. These are ex-pros and semi-pros and they're not going to take kindly to having some young kid running rings around them and scoring goals.' He couldn't have been more on the money.

Sure enough, during the game that day, a chance fell for me on the edge of the box and as I was about to shoot, one of the Chorley players cleaned me out completely and that was the end of my afternoon – and the end of my season yet again. I knew it was bad because shock set in almost straight away and I was cold and shivery. I was helped over to the bench and sat with Tony Book who asked how I was, and I just told him it was sore.

When we went into the dressing room, he told me to get a shower, but I said I couldn't because I was freezing. 'I've broken my leg, Skip,' I said. He said he thought that I hadn't. He asked if it was about this time the previous year that I broke my leg with Bolton Lads. I told him it was about a year to the day, there or thereabouts. Skip said, 'Lightning doesn't strike twice, you'll be fine.' Everyone always seemed to know better than me!

He got some of the lads to help me get dressed and he called my mum and asked her to come and collect me as he wasn't sure what was best to do, so she drove to Chorley and took me to the hospital in Bolton where the X-rays showed the same fracture as last year had opened up again. It was a spiral fracture of my right shin bone, and I went to see the specialist a few days after. He had last year's all-clear X-rays next to the ones I'd just had done. He said it was like déjà vu. He couldn't believe it and said that he'd never seen anything like it before.

He told me that the shin had healed so he couldn't understand why it had opened up again. Successive Decembers in plaster, and people ask me today why I don't like Christmas!

Two or three weeks later, my old coach from Bolton Lads, Billy Howarth, came around and was talking to my dad when he said, 'Is that him done with football then?' I turned around and said, 'No way!' In many ways, that was a sort of turning point for our household. Nobody could believe I'd had the same break on the same weekend as the last year, and after Billy left, my dad said, 'You know, you have to have a think about it – we need to consider whether your legs are made for football or not. Do you want to carry on because you know how hard it was last year?'

I said that we had England youth physio Craig Simmons in our corner now and that I'd come back strong before and could do it again. I wasn't packing it in. No chance.

8

Broken Dreams?

NEWS OF my latest injury gradually filtered through to England, and Craig Simmons called me to see how I was and then set up an exercise plan to increase my upper-body strength over the next 16 weeks. England kept in touch by sending letters to keep up with my progress. Can you imagine that today? Letters! It was akin to the Pony Express, but that's how it was back then. I had no doubts in my mind. I wanted to be a footballer and that's all I wanted to do.

Things had been opening up for me and I was never going to toss it all away unless it got to a stage where I physically couldn't play anymore and had absolutely no choice. I was training with City and was an England Schoolboys/youth regular – I'd worked hard to get to this stage and as far as I was concerned, everything was in front of me.

It was difficult to swallow, but I'd done it before and I could do it again and, after getting over the first month where

I did feel pretty low, devastated even, I started to focus on the future again and my natural determination kicked in.

My dad kept me off school for the first few weeks to make sure I didn't slip or fall and make the leg any worse, and then the council helped out by paying for a taxi to take me to school in the mornings and then take me home again afterwards, just the same as they had done the previous year. Other than that, I was pretty much housebound; the weather was cold and often icy so I couldn't take any chances outside.

I didn't go to watch Bolton Lads or City until my leg came out of plaster and I had the chance to go and watch City take on United at Old Trafford in the Lancashire Youth Cup Final four days later. It was a Saturday morning and me and my grandad got a lift to the ground. After, we walked all the way to the East Lancs Road which was a good one or two-mile walk – and my ankle and shin were so sore after that. It was too much, too soon and my whole leg felt sore. That was the first time I'd had doubts about whether I'd recover from this latest break, but I put a few bags of ice on it when I got home, and it was fine.

Towards the back end of the season, I started playing again for Bolton Lads and was fit enough to play in the Lancashire Cup Final. We'd drawn the first two games, but I managed to get fit for the second replay and scored twice to help us win it. We were the only team in the history of the competition to win it at under-14 and under-16 – a record we are all still proud of. This was my sign-off for the Lads Club.

City had kept in touch with my dad, and I was never in any doubt that Tony Book, Glyn Pardoe, Ken Barnes and Roy Bailey only had my best interests – and the other lads' in the City youth team – at heart.

In fact, I was about to learn that first-team manager Billy McNeill was also keeping close tabs on my progress – only this time I would be gutted that he'd taken such close interest in me.

I'd been to Lilleshall to see physio Craig Simmons during the summer months, and he was once again amazed at my recovery. I did a series of tests with him including some timed running sessions that he told me were as good as they'd been before the injury. Satisfied with my fitness, I received a letter from the FA soon after inviting me to join the England under-17 squad for a tournament in Cannes (I was a year young, too). I couldn't have been happier and was excited at the prospect of playing for England again. They had to inform City of my call-up as well and when they did, Tony Book phoned my dad and told him Billy McNeill wanted to speak to him and me later that evening if it was OK.

I started wondering if I might be in for a first-team opportunity or similar and all sorts of stuff was going around in my head – but the last thing I was expecting was what

McNeill said, which was along the lines of, 'Look, you've broke your leg twice in less than two years, we don't think you're ready for this, so you're not going.'

That was the end of that, as I couldn't go against City's wishes, but I understood why McNeill had said what he did, even if I didn't agree with it. They were looking after mine and the club's interests – but I was gutted. At least, by July, I was able to start as a full-time apprentice with City, which included daily training sessions and regular matches in the Lancashire League and the FA Youth and Lancashire Youth Cup.

I'd left school and was now a first-year YTS. It meant I had to be up and out of the house for about 7.10am each morning, get a lift to near the train station, then a short walk to catch the train to Manchester and then it was a bus to Princess Parkway bus depot in Moss Side and then a one-mile walk to Maine Road.

Gary Jackson was one of City's most promising young players, who was there or thereabouts with the first team, but I couldn't get over how he took me under his wing and looked after me. He would give me lifts to the train or sometimes home to Bolton and I was thinking, as I got in his Saab-sponsored club car, 'I've finally arrived!'

I hadn't of course, but another top club believed I was well on my way to fulfilling the promise I'd shown as a kid and would be about to test City's belief in me.

9

'Name Your Price for Moulden'

THE 1984/85 season began positively for me. My sole focus now was making it at City and, if England under-17s or whatever came calling, so much the better. I'd always backed myself and whenever I'd moved up a level, the goals had kept on coming.

Pre-season went really well, and I was looking to really get going. Hard work had never scared me, and I was an athletic lad, so I threw myself into the training and fitness schedule, but I suppose because I'd had three broken legs over the past six years it had cost me more than two years of football, so I was always looking to make the most of it when I was fit.

I remember during one session at Manchester University playing fields just off the M60, Billy McNeill was putting the first team through their paces. They trained in an all-green kit, but when they came to do a game, they realised nobody had brought the bibs out. Billy shouted me over as he knew me from the running sessions I'd done with him the season before and said, 'You're fast, aren't you? Go back to the dressing rooms and get the bibs for me.'

It was about a mile away, so I set off, grabbed the bibs and sprinted back, and as I got nearer, I could see Tony Book and Billy shaking their heads. As I arrived and handed them over, I understood why they had shaken their heads. I'd brought green bibs out for the green kit they were playing in. I got deservedly hammered for that.

Chris Coleman, a lad from South Wales, had done pre-season as a new apprentice like we were – and what a player he was. He stayed with us for a few weeks and Christ, that lad could play. But he was homesick, and nothing could cure that, so he went back to Swansea and, of course, went on to have a fantastic career with Swansea, Fulham and Wales. What a talent, and he could have done it all with Manchester City had things been different.

I had one minor setback as the season neared, when I pulled my hamstring and was sidelined for two or three weeks. It was one of the first soft tissue injuries I'd had and would be almost the only one I suffered in my whole career, but it was enough to keep me out of the first City A team league game.

We had a strong squad with John Beresford, Paul Simpson, Jamie Hoyland, Jason and Darren Beckford, Ricky Adams and Eric Nixon among the group. We all used to call Eric

'Eric the Viking' (among other things!) and he was a handful, and what a character. He was a muscular 22-year-old and in the changing rooms, he'd stand there naked in the swan pose. Then he'd flick the light off and grab whoever was closest and give them a dead arm. Everyone kept their arms down their sides when the lights went out. He was mad as a hatter, but he was actually a really great lad.

My regular task as a YTS was to clean the dressing rooms and pick the kit up – that was my small part each session.

From that season, there are a few memories I have that stick out, the first being a repeat of City's famous Ballet on Ice against Spurs in 1967, albeit on a less grand scale! We were away to Alsager with the A team, and it was a rock-hard pitch that the referee surprisingly passed as playable.

We were all sat ready to go out in our moulded soles and after the referee came in to inspect us, Tony Book then told us to switch to our leather studs. We did, and we removed the top layer from them. That left three small but barely visible pins showing, which we went out and played with, and while we were all able to play as though it was a normal grass pitch, the Alsager lads were like pigs on ice. Apparently Tony had given the same advice back in 1967 and City had gone on to win 4-1. It was an eye-opener, as so many things were back then, and while it wasn't cheating, it was stretching the rules maybe. And I'm not saying a club like Manchester City had to bend the rules to beat Alsager College – it was always about being able to give your best performance, preparation and representing the club as best as possible.

However, if you're going to switch your studs, you've got to remember to switch them back after the game. I didn't, and I wore the same boots for a training session a couple of days later and sliced Jason Beckford's hand open by accident after I went after a high ball. I thought I'd get a right bollocking, but under the circumstances it was brushed under the carpet pretty quickly.

Sorry about that, Jason!

As mentioned earlier, the Lancashire League was that odd mix of experienced pros, kids and semi-professionals with universities, non-league sides and top-division clubs. You never knew what you'd be up against next, but it was never dull and a great place to learn your trade.

Occasionally I'd get the odd reserve-team game as well that season and, every now and then, you'd come up against some well-known names who were on their way back from injury.

My first reserve game was memorable for the argument in the changing rooms between Ray Ranson and Billy McNeill. Billy was furious at Ray for something or other and he called Tony Book in – I don't think Tony wanted to get involved, but he didn't have a choice. It was like your mum and dad arguing. So this argument was raging on, and the senior pros told all the young lads to stay where they were in the bath and keep out of the argument, which we did. Then we spotted a turd in the water and my money was on Nicky Reid – but no one ever owned up to it!

For my first few games, Ray Ranson was a fantastic help and was always advising me and talking to me through matches. He said he would always be an out if I needed it, and if I was in doubt, pass it back to him. It doesn't sound like much, but when you're starting out, it was good, solid and comforting advice from somebody who had a lot of first-team experience. I played against West Bromwich Albion for my first reserve game and my second was against Coventry City.

In the Coventry game I would be up against Brian 'Killer' Kilcline, who was about five years older than me and had played about 250 league games for Notts County and the Sky Blues. I thought, 'Right, here we go,' but Tony Book told me that this was what big boys' football was all about, and just to go out and keep Kilcline and the ball moving. Nothing too in-depth, just simple words that got you thinking about what you should be doing.

In the game, Killer called me a 'little fucker' a couple of times, but in a jokey way. Years later at Oldham Athletic, Brian told me he remembered that evening really well. He said he'd gone out for a nice stroll to build his fitness up but that I'd ran the bollocks off him! Brian is a true gentleman.

Then I was up against Notts County for City reserves where I had Pedro Richards marking me. He was around 28 then and had something like 400 games under his belt in league football. County had put most of their first team out and I did well against Pedro – so much so that Billy McNeill came into the changing rooms afterwards to say so and told me he thought I was nearing the standard that was needed to be considered for City's first team. It made me feel brilliant. It felt like things were at last clicking into place. I also played against Kenny Burns when he was at Barnsley and held my own and got a pat on the back after the game. I couldn't believe it – he'd held up the European Cup for Nottingham Forest!

But everything was about to get a bit surreal.

Me and Darren Beckford returned to Maine Road after playing for England under-17s at Fulham's Craven Cottage, where we did well as we always did when we played together. What we weren't expecting was what happened next.

I remember Billy McNeill calling Darren and myself into his office and he said to me, 'You get the train home, don't you?' I said yes, and he went on, 'Well, you'll see something on your way back, but just ignore it all.'

I set off home after training and wondered what the hell he'd been on about. Then, when I got off the bus in town, the story McNeill was warning me about was plastered on the *Manchester Evening News* billboards on my way back to Victoria Station. They read, 'Tottenham tell City to name a price for Beckford and Moulden.' Apparently, Spurs had offered a blank cheque to sign us both, but McNeill was having none of it and had told us not to worry because we were going nowhere.

It was bizarre. I'd had two years of being mostly in the doldrums with broken legs, working on getting back fit and then, all of a sudden, everything was happening. My head was spinning. But why would I want to go anywhere else? I'd just signed for City, and they were the club I wanted to play for. I'd come to that conclusion after going to several clubs, and nothing had changed, so why would I swap Manchester City for Tottenham? I wasn't going to go to my agent and say I wanted to leave because I didn't have one. But I would never have done that anyway.

It was all about getting my head down, working hard and getting on with it and, at that time, the FA Youth Cup was our main target.

Our hopes of any silverware were ended on Tyneside, however, as we crashed out away to Newcastle United. We'd fancied our chances as we'd reached the quarter-finals but were maybe a year too young thinking back.

It was a freezing night and a rock-hard pitch, but the game went ahead, as they tended to back then. The referee couldn't make it so George Courtney stepped in as he lived nearby in Spennymoor. He was a top-flight ref with a reputation for being somewhat controversial. The game shouldn't have been played but because both teams were there and we had an official, we played it. Earl Barrett brought Joe Allen down and Paul Gascoigne scored a back-post header from the resulting free kick to give Newcastle a 1-0 win on the night.

You could tell Gazza was a real talent – anyone could see that – but we were gutted. One thing I learned that night was that in football at that level, everything mattered. Billy McNeill had travelled to the north-east to watch and he proper kicked off afterwards with Mr Courtney, saying the game should never have been played and the free kick that the goal came from should never have been given. For me, it was like 'Wow! This is big-time football.'

If you got a good result, you could travel home with any family members who had come to watch rather than them having to meet the coach in Manchester, but that night I had to get the coach.

We ended the season by winning the Lancashire Youth Cup and League, but the season after, everything finally clicked into place for our age group. Paul Lake and Andy Hinchcliffe were two of the lads who joined, and we had a team that gelled on and off the pitch.

In my last year at primary school, St Osmond's

The infamous Lads Club team at Under-12s

Broken leg number two: Mum, me, Helen and Lisa (girlfriend)

The weekend before starting our YTS at City. Me, Ian Scott, Dave White and Ste Crompton

First year YTS in 1984/85. Playing for the 'A' team at Platt Lane

Eric Mullender, me, dad, posing for the Bolton Evening News

Linda Curl of Norwich Ladies scored 22 goals in a 40–0 league victory over Milton Keynes Reserves at Norwich on 25 Sept 1983.

The greatest number of goals in a season reported for an individual player in junior professional league football is 96 by Tom Duffy (b. 7 Jan 1937), who played centre forward for Ardeer Thistle FC, Strathclyde in the 1960–1 season. Paul Anthony Moulden (b. 6 Sept 1967) scored 289 goals in 40 games for Bolton Lads Club in Bolton Boys Federation intermediate league and cup matches in 1981–2. An additional 51 goals scored in other tournaments brought his total to 340, the highest season figure reported in any class of competitive football for an individual.

Wind-aided goals in 3 sec after kick-off have been scored by a number of players. Tony Bacon, of Schalmont HS scored three goals *v.* Icabod Crane HS in 63 sec at Schenectady, New York, USA on 8 Oct 1975.

I'm with Franz Carr (just before he moved to Nottingham Forest) in Russia, playing for Young England

One of my early goals, getting congratulated by Tony Grealish

Scoring against Brighton – no waving to the Kippax – after Skip's little chat two years previous

With Paul Stewart and Paul Simpson.

With Joyce Johnstone, laundry lady at Manchester City for years

A great pic! Andy Hinchcliffe, Paul Lake, Dave White, Ian Brightwell, me and Ste Redmond

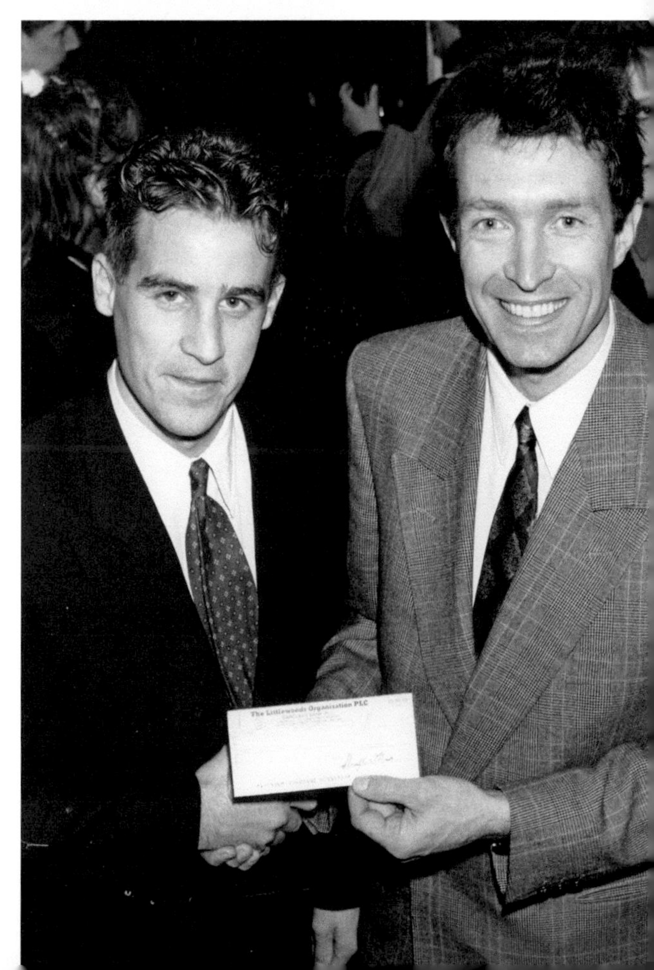

Receiving a cheque for scoring three against Sheffield United. It went to Bolton Ladies' Club, to Jerry Glover who was leader of the club back in the day

*Now you see me,
now you don't*

I started the 1985/86 season by travelling to Russia with England for the FIFA World Youth Championship at the end of August and start of September, but most of our really good players weren't available because they were playing first-team football, so we failed miserably, going out at the group stage after drawing one and losing twice for our three matches.

It was another good experience, being away with my country at the age of 17 and playing in an under-23 tournament, but it wasn't very fulfilling, especially with the knowledge that we could have probably won it if we had all of our best players there.

I was supremely fit – in fact, I reckon only two players in my career were fitter than me, namely Ian Brightwell and Neil Redfearn. I think I was probably on a par with Brighty, but there weren't many others who could match our level.

It was still Glyn Pardoe and Tony Book in charge and for most second-year YTS players, our target was now getting into City's reserve team and, for me, I wanted to stay part of the England youth team.

John Beresford had Darren Beckford moved up to the reserves and Ricky Adams had retired but we had Ian Scott, Brighty, Steve Redmond, David White, David Boyd, Paul Lake and Andy Hinchcliffe.

Jason Beckford was a couple of years younger and still part of the schoolboy teams at City, but he was always around and involved. He also did the best impersonation of Tony Book I ever heard. It was unbelievable. One day, he was getting changed and we were all in together and I shouted over, 'Becky! Give us a Booky!' So, he stood up on the bench and he shouted – in a perfect gravelly West Country growl – 'Hey Glyn! What's up with herrrr? Come on lads!'

Of course, Booky had by this point appeared in the doorway while Becky carried on. He probably sussed something was up as we were laughing and then sort of turned the other way. Becky turned to his left to see Tony Book stood there and it was the first time I ever saw a black lad go bright red. Booky took it fantastically well and said, 'That's not bad that, Becky. Get your spikes on, lad.' If you ever heard that shout, you knew you were in for an exhausting running session. That's what he ended up with that day. Jason was shit hot, what a player, but like me, injuries would dominate his future career.

In November 1985, I was finally given my first-team debut in the Full Members' Cup at home to Sunderland. I was 17, and I'd been sent over to train with the first team a few days before to take part in a five-a-side game. Billy McNeill was a very hands-on manager and always around, and he'd always let you know that he was keeping an eye on you with a 'you played well yesterday' comment or similar every now and then. It would never be a long conversation, but he'd always make you feel wanted and let you know he was aware of everything.

John Beresford also got the nod to go over and train and I was named on the bench.

The competition wasn't that popular as a whole, with less than 7,000 inside Maine Road, but I didn't care. This was what I'd been waiting for.

I came on with a short time to go, we drew 2-2, and then it was down to a penalty shoot-out. Skipper Kenny Clements said, 'Make yourself a name – go and take one.'

I was well up for taking a penalty and went over to Billy McNeill to put my name down, but he said, 'Nah, you're not taking one.' I think he wanted to protect me in case I missed, but I was as confident as I always was and fancied it. We won 4-2 on penalties as it happened and progressed to the next round. As for me, I'd played for City's first team. Less than two years before, I was running out at Hacken Lane for Bolton Lads, so it was still a bit surreal, but this was everything I'd worked for and, in spite of three bad leg breaks, it had really happened. Best of all, I knew I could do it and hold my own at senior football level. What could possibly go wrong?

10

The Golden Generation

OUR YOUTH team were ridiculously good, and we were regularly hammering teams in the Lancashire League. We could feel it was going to be a special year and it was embarrassing how good our football was. There were no weaknesses with most of us in or around the reserve side plus a few who had played for the first team. What we wanted more than anything was to win the FA Youth Cup. As most of us were on our second year as a YTS, we knew that this would be our last chance to win it before we were either given a pro contract or released.

We cruised through the early rounds, often turning sides over in the Lancashire League. Around Christmas, I was being included in the matchday squad as the notorious 13th man. That pretty much was reserved for a young player to blood them into the ways of the senior team and experience what it was like being part of the first team. I think Earl

Barrett was 13th man for something like 13 matches on the spin, then it was Darren Beckford and now it seemed to be me.

A few of the lads were taking the mick because it was coming up to Christmas and most of the youth team would have a few days off then, whereas the first team would have more games than ever, but it was what I had worked hard for and, as I said, I didn't like Christmas anyway!

A few weeks before, we'd played Aston Villa's reserves at Maine Road and I was up against the old warhorse Alan Evans who was just on his way back from injury. In the first few minutes I remember the ball being played into me by Paul Simpson just outside the box and Evans launched into me with a tackle that sent me about ten feet into the air – and I didn't even have the ball!

I looked around and Evans said, 'Calm down, lad. There's going to be no runabout tonight, is there?'

What he meant was, we had a reputation for being pacy with good movement and he didn't want to be chasing shadows looking a dick all night as he continued his recovery. It was another little snapshot of what life in men's football was all about.

Fast forward a fortnight and I was included in the 13-man squad for the away game with Villa on New Year's Day 1986. We had to be at Maine Road for the team coach for 8am but I spun my Vauxhall Cavalier at the roundabout on Princess

Parkway on the way to the ground. It was frosty and icy in patches and though I didn't hit anything, I did a complete spin around and it was like, 'What the fuck's going on here?'

I got to the ground, got on the bus and we picked up the majority of the players at the roundabout near the Four Seasons Hotel at Hale Barnes before heading off for the hotel near Villa Park where we'd have our pre-match meal.

I was sat with a few of the younger lads who had only been in the first team for a year or less and when my dinner arrived, it was chicken and beans. If you weren't playing, you got chips as well, so when Jim Melrose saw his plate had chips on, he said to the server, 'I think you've got this wrong – his is the one with chips,' nodding at me. Our meals had come alphabetically so it was Melrose then Moulden, and Billy McNeill shouted over, 'No, that's bang on, Jim.'

It stopped me in my tracks as that meant I was going to make my league debut against Aston Villa – or at least be sub – and I could hardly put the fork in my mouth I was shaking that much. After we'd finished, McNeill came over and said, 'Have you worked it out? You're making your debut, today.'

I thanked him and tried to get myself mentally prepared. One of the jobs of the 13th man was to change anyone's studs who wanted them changing on the day of the game. As it was a kid's role, I knew Jim Melrose wasn't going to do that, so when Andy May wanted his changing, I just told him I would sort it.

Andy, Gary Jackson and a few of the fringe first-team players were great lads, but one or two of the regulars could be quite harsh. Graham Baker was fantastic, and I don't think I'd have done half as well as I did when I played for the seniors if it wasn't for Baker. He just told me to make the runs and the ball would be with me. Tony Grealish was another wise head who taught me a lot about being a professional footballer, as did Sammy McIlroy, even if some of that was during reserve matches. They were just happy to impart good, solid advice as Ray Ranson had done – but Ray was being frozen out for whatever reason at the time.

The game against Villa ended 1-0 to us and I played the full 90 minutes wearing the number nine jersey. Everything was so fast, but I managed to keep pace and it was a step up again. At the end of the match, everyone seemed fairly happy with my contribution, and it felt good.

Afterwards, my dad said, 'How was that?' I told him it was quick, so he asked me what it had been like when I first trained with City. I said 'quick' again. Then he asked what it had been like when I first played for England Schoolboys and the answer again was 'quick'. The reserves for the first time? 'Quick.' He then said that I'd soon get used to it, it was all about adjusting and hopefully I'd go from strength to strength.

I must have done enough against Villa because three days later I was on the bench for our FA Cup third-round tie away to Walsall and was disappointed not to start, but then I pinched myself and reminded myself how far I'd come already. I came on for Gordon Davies with about 15 minutes to go and we won 3-1, but the thing I remember most about that day was my feet were freezing. When I did come on, I felt like I had blocks of ice on the ends of my legs, but again, I did enough to get a few positive comments from Billy McNeill and some of the other lads afterwards. But just when things were starting to take off, so the bad luck kicked back in.

Televised five-a-side tournaments were huge at the time, with the BBC's *Sportsnight* showing different competitions that most of the big clubs would enter. Whether it was in London, Birmingham or wherever, you'd get sell-out crowds of around 10,000 and sides made up of first-team regulars with everyone keen to win it.

I was included in City's team to play in the Scottish Fives up in Glasgow and was thrilled to be part of something I'd been watching on TV for several years. But it proved to be a bit of a disaster.

Incredibly, during one of the games, the ball was played across the D of the five-a-side pitch to me and, as I went to slide it home, my foot caught the edge of the synthetic pitch covering and rolled it back like a carpet, causing me to do the splits; I had immediate pain in my groin and side. My tournament ended there and then and when I got back to Manchester, the club specialist Sydney Rose diagnosed a hernia and booked me in for an op at the end of the season. It was bad timing to say the least.

The highlight of that season was undoubtedly the FA Youth Cup and I remember us travelling to face Fulham at Craven Cottage in the quarter-finals. The first team were playing Chelsea that day and had gone down the night before, but we had to travel on the day of the game. I remember thinking that we should have been the ones who went overnight as we had a real chance of winning something prestigious whereas the first team were always going to get beat at Stamford Bridge. They lost 1-0 and we beat Fulham, but I probably had my worst game in a City shirt and one of the worst I could ever recall at any level. I haven't got a clue what went on that day, but it still stands out in my memory even today. We weren't anywhere near our best as a team, but Paul Lake scored the only goal and that meant we were in the semi-final against Arsenal in mid-April. A fixture congestion had threatened what had felt like our procession towards winning the competition for the first time, but Arsenal were probably the biggest threat left.

They had a good side, with Michael Thomas, Nicky Hammond, Roger Stanislaus, Adrian Pennington and Paul

Merson among their number. We travelled down to Highbury, and it was like a different world, with a big marble reception area, really smart dressing rooms and a genuine feel of history around the place. There was a slight slope on the pitch but we acquitted ourselves well and gave as good as we got, although we lost 1-0.

But ahead of that, Tony Book taught me a valuable lesson. We were due to play Southport in the Lancashire League a couple of days after Arsenal as we couldn't get any of the fixtures in between postponed. So it was a cold Saturday morning in Southport and memories of my broken leg against Chorley a couple of years earlier were in the back of my mind. Our squad was small, and we only had a pool of about 16 players to choose from, so that meant we pretty much had to play continuously.

But there was a side story to this game – a couple, in fact. About ten years earlier, my dad had been playing in the Bolton Hospital Cup, which was a big deal in Bolton and open to each and every club in the town. It was a way of raising funds for the main hospital in Bolton as a cap would be taken around each game and people would put in what they could. The final was at Burnden Park and the teams that entered were serious about winning it.

In this particular game, I was sat around four feet from the pitch on a railway sleeper and this lad did my dad with a late tackle. My dad got up and smacked him and there was uproar on the sidelines. The referee came over and said, 'Did you just hit him?' My dad said, 'I'm an ex-pro, I don't do things like that.'

The lad in question was by now at Southport and by now was an old semi-pro. My dad knew this, and he told me that if the lad was playing, he'd know who I was, and as certain as God made little apples, he'd try and do me to get some payback for all those years ago. On the day of the game, I looked at the team sheet and sure enough, he was playing.

I wasn't being big-headed, but I didn't attach much importance to that game because I think we were well clear at the top anyway, so even though that guy didn't get near me, another Southport defender had been giving me a bit of a kicking throughout the first half. I just wanted to get through it and come out the other side having not picked up an injury and be ready for the second leg against Arsenal.

At half-time we went into the dressing room and Tony Book laid into me. He came up to me and was about three inches from my face, shouting, 'You? All you're interested in is not getting injured today. He's kicking lumps out of you and that's all you're bothered about? Get your boots off and get in the shower!' Skip could read you like a book, but he wasn't finished. It was deadly quiet, and I looked around and figured we didn't have a sub, so wondered if we were going to go out there with ten men in the second half. But Skip had other ideas.

He said, 'Pass me those shorts, Glyn.' He took his tracksuit bottoms off and put the shorts on, put some socks and boots on – no shin pads – and everyone was like, 'What the fuck is going on?' It was like a scene from the film *Kes*, only nobody was laughing.

Skip, by then 51 years old, ran out for the second half and Glyn said, 'Forget the shower, come outside and watch this.' Within five minutes, Skip – playing at centre-forward – let the lad who'd been kicking me get the ball in the corner before coming in from behind and scissor-tackling him. The guy had to be stretchered off! Skip came over to the bench and said to me, 'That's how you sort them out!' It was a huge lesson for me, and I knew I'd let Skip and Glyn down massively that day. To me, it had only been a Lancashire League game, but to them it really mattered, and it made me realise that every time I went out to play, I had to be on it and give my everything. That's what it would take to get to the very top.

I was selected for the second leg against Arsenal, and I knew I had to deliver. I couldn't vindicate what I'd done, but if I could be the difference and turn the tie in our favour, then it would be going part of the way to mending any damage I'd done. I'd known Michael Thomas for about three years, and I saw him looking around in the foyer as he came into Maine

Road, comparing it to Highbury. But this was my back yard, and I wasn't going to let him or anyone else from Arsenal look down their noses at us, so outside the dressing room I told Mickey that they were going to have it.

They went ahead but I scored twice to make it 2-1 on the night and 2-2 on aggregate, meaning it went to penalties. My second goal was one of the best I ever scored. I stuck my penalty home and we won 5-4 to progress to the final where we'd be playing Manchester United over two legs. We wanted United and we'd beaten them regularly over the past few seasons and knew we were better than them.

We didn't have long to prepare for the game due to the fixture backlog. The first leg at Old Trafford was just two days later so we went into Maine Road the following day and Glyn, Skip and Roy Bailey had placed these boards across the big bath and were giving us all rub-downs. The first-teamers would occasionally put their heads around and take the piss, but you could see how much this mattered to our coaches and the club. For Roy, Skip, Glyn and Ken Barnes, this was massive and the culmination of years of hard graft. Their reputations for excellence in youth football were at stake and though we didn't get that at the time, I understand it better now. They were hard taskmasters, but every lad from that era loved them to bits.

If we won the FA Youth Cup, it sent out a statement that if you were a talented kid looking for a club where you would be developed, you wouldn't go far wrong if you chose Manchester City, so that's what we were playing for. There was no pressure on us to win – just to go out, work hard and give a good account of ourselves, get the ball down and play. That was the only criteria we had and 48 hours after the Arsenal game, we walked out at Old Trafford to face United in the first leg.

The pitch was shite and suited them better than us, and though we secured a 1-1 draw, I was devastated because we'd smashed them time and time again. They weren't bad players but they weren't on our level. I couldn't sleep that night because I couldn't believe they'd actually given us a game.

The second leg at Maine Road proved a lot more popular than I think the club had anticipated. There had been about 6,000 at Old Trafford so the plan was to only open up the Main Stand, but the Kippax and Platt Lane Stand had to be opened as well as more than 18,000 turned up. Oh, how I miss the Kippax!

I set the first goal up, sending a cross in from the corner of the box and David Boyd came from nowhere to thump a thunderous header home – one of the best I'd ever seen – and give us a 1-0 lead. I didn't know he could even head it, never mind head a goal like that. United clung in there, but with eight minutes to go Ian Scott's shot was spilled by Gary Walsh and I'd read it. As I set off, my legs were giving way in the sandy goalmouth at Maine Road but I just managed to get there first and managed to squeeze it over the line to make it 2-0 and that was that. We'd finally won the FA Youth Cup and done it against United at Maine Road, so it was an unbelievable feeling and a landmark moment for our club.

Despite our success, we still had our apprentice work to do to keep our feet on the ground, and one particular job would leave today's academy players with their mouths open if they were asked to do it. Thinking back, it was one of the most bizarre undertakings I had in my whole career.

Monday morning after a Saturday game at Maine Road meant a trip to the bank, but not to withdraw our meagre salaries – it was to take the entire gate receipts for the first team's match! It was one of five or six jobs we had on Mondays, but this one sticks out because there would be piles of cash and coins tipped into a trolley that four of us – in our full City training kit – would then take to the Co-op Bank in the centre of Manchester. Imagine, if we'd had a gate of say 30,000, the receipts could be up to £40,000 or more and we were taking that in a club Saab which had its nose pointed up to the sky with the weight in the boot.

We were sitting ducks and stuck out like a sore thumb – my dad said it was a minor miracle nobody ever pulled a gun or knife on us to steal the money, but we did it because we were apprentices and thought nothing of it. It was crazy, but typical of how the club worked at that point.

So, that was that for 1985/86 and the season was finally over – my last as an apprentice and from here on in, it was all about trying to get into that first team and do what I did best – score goals.

While most of my mates in the youth team headed off on holidays abroad, for me it was surgery time.

I went under the knife to try and sort the hernia issue out on 29 May 1986, but the surgeon, Mr Rose, then told me he hadn't been able to find any hernia issues. The injury I actually had, which wouldn't be correctly diagnosed by any surgeon for years to come, was a hip impingement.

Here's a medical description of the problem I had:

'Hip impingement, or femoroacetabular impingement (FAI), occurs when the femoral head (ball of the hip) pinches up against the acetabulum (cup of the hip). When this happens, damage to the labrum (cartilage that surrounds the acetabulum) can occur, causing hip stiffness and pain, and can lead to arthritis.'

So the rolled-up carpet at the Scottish Fives had given me a whole new issue to deal with and I wouldn't play again for a couple of months while the injury settled. It was another case of one step forward, two steps back. It would be 14 weeks before I played for City again. I also missed playing in the Full Members' Cup Final, even though I was part of the squad that lost 5-4 to Chelsea in front of almost 70,000 at Wembley. How's your luck, Mouldy?

11

Going Down

CITY TRAVELLED to Sweden in pre-season, though I was still building my fitness up while we were playing friendlies.

Jimmy Frizzell, Billy McNeill's number two, was somebody I had a lot of time for. He'd done brilliantly during his time as Oldham Athletic boss and was a really good guy. Jimmy's knees and hips were so bad. In five-a-side games he'd curse anyone who didn't play the ball to his feet as he was so stiff that he didn't have the flexibility to chase passes. 'To feet, to feet for fuck's sake!' he used to yell in that gentle Scottish accent.

And it was while we were in Sweden, I thought Eric Nixon had killed him. We went white-water rafting on a team-bonding day and, along the way, Eric the Viking decided it would be a good idea if he chucked the 50-year-old Jimmy out of the boat. Jimmy went under the water and then under the boat. All we could see was the bald patch on the top of his head with his combover floating up and I thought he was literally dead in the water, but we somehow dragged him out. When he recovered, he gave Eric an almighty bollocking because his glasses were on the riverbed somewhere about eight feet below.

I honestly couldn't catch my breath I was laughing so hard, but the main thing was he was OK in the end and the possibility of Eric facing a manslaughter charge was no longer on the cards. How Jimmy survived, God only knows.

The 1986/87 season got off to the worst possible start when Billy McNeill quit after a month. He left for Aston Villa, probably because City were skint and he could see the writing on the wall, but I was sorry to see him go as he had always shown interest in my progress and was a good man-manager.

That meant Jimmy Frizzell was given the job, so at least there was some continuity. I was included for the games against Southend in the League Cup and Leicester in the league, but I didn't score in either.

Against Southampton, I came off the bench and Jimmy told me to go and sort out Mark Dennis. Anyone who knows Mark Dennis knows his disciplinary record was appalling and he was pretty much a walking red card – a proper hard lad – at a time when referees didn't flash cards around like they do today. Jimmy put me at outside-right and in direct opposition to Dennis, but I managed to hold my own and survive the time I was on.

My schoolboy record and goals for the youth and reserve teams meant that I was starting to feel a bit of pressure as the games passed, because I'd always scored at every level and, now, I was eight appearances into my senior career, and I still hadn't found the back of the net.

Then, at last, the goals began to come.

I was named in the starting XI to face the Crazy Gang – Wimbledon – in a home Full Members' Cup tie in front of around 5,000 Maine Road fans. It would end up being an eventful evening and something of a learning curve for me as I received the biggest bollocking of my life.

I would score two goals in a 3-1 win, the first a diving header and the second a bicycle kick that flew past Dave Beasant into the roof of the net. I put in a good shift, but I should have had a hat-trick as I had a good chance late on, but I was knackered and, as the ball came to me, I reckon my mum could have hit it harder in her stilettos. After that, Wimbledon immediately went up the other end and almost scored themselves, but we kept them out.

At the end of the game as I started to walk off the pitch, some of our fans on the Kippax had started singing my name, so I acknowledged them by clapping back at them as I headed towards the dugout. As I looked at our bench, I could feel

Tony Book's eyes boring into me and I was thinking, 'What the hell have I done here?' The look he gave me was one of utter disgust and disdain, so I knew I was in for it – but for what, I had no clue.

In the dressing room, Frizz gave his post-match talk and when he'd finished, Skip just looked over at me and said, 'You.' I thought, 'Here we go.' After a Lancashire League game against Chester the year before, the whole team got a royal bollocking from Skip that we later called 'The Carlsberg Bollocking' because it was probably the best bollocking we would ever have!

So I thought, anyway. By the time Skip had finished ranting at me, the rest of the players had washed and left, so the captain Kenny Clements came over and said, 'Skip, leave it. You've said enough now.'

I don't think Skip could have said anything more in all honesty, but the gist of his anger was that I'd taken a shot instead of running the ball into the corner and keeping possession. He said the worst thing I could have done was to take shot because, within three passes, they'd had a header on our goal.

His main beef, however, was me clapping the Kippax. So, I'd gone from scoring two goals, missing another, and then clapping the fans and in the space of that one minute – all my good work had been undone in his eyes.

Skip was so big on managing egos and us not getting ahead of ourselves, and he said, 'When you've played 250 games for this club and scored 200 goals, then you can clap the Kippax. Until then, I don't want to ever see you doing that again.' That was me told!

He was, as always, bang on and I respected him. He'd taken maybe 20 minutes too long to tell me, but I knew why he was doing it.

I got into a cold bath and, afterwards, my dad told me on the drive home that I'd done well, but I just sat there quiet and didn't tell him what had gone on with Skip, probably because I didn't want my dad's disapproval. He probably thought I was sulking because I hadn't scored more!

Despite the bollocking I took, I was finally off the mark, and I kept my place for the next game against Aston Villa a few days later in the league. Villa were Billy McNeill's team now, of course, but on their journey to Maine Road that day their coach was in a fatal collision. I remember that clearly.

I scored twice more. The first was a mistake by the Villa defence that gave me a chance close in that I tapped or headed home – I can't recall which – and as I ran back to the halfway line, I realised that it wasn't that different from reserve football. People still made mistakes and I just felt a bit of a weight lifted off me because I was thinking I might do all right at this level. The second goal was a turn and shot into the top-left corner from 20 yards and we went on to win 3-1. I was starting to feel part of everything, and that things were heading in the right direction.

Another goal in the next game – a 2-1 win over Charlton Athletic – meant we'd won three on the bounce and I'd scored five goals in three matches, but the decision by the club to fly off to Saudi Arabia the day after Charlton was bonkers. We travelled over there for about five days where we had a game against the Saudi national team during what I think was British Expo week. The travelling and the heat were unbearable and we flew directly back to London on the Friday ahead of our league game against Arsenal. It had been a nightmare of a trip, and the fact that we were awful against Arsenal was only to be expected because we were all exhausted. We lost 3-0 at Highbury, but I would keep my place, scoring the only goal in a 1-0 win over Watford in the Full Members' Cup. Then Frizz asked if I could play up front on my own against defending champions Everton. I was happy to do that because I loved having space where I could make my own runs on either side, and I was looking forward to it.

I'd been to Everton as a kid and they were the benchmark at the time, so to score my seventh goal in six games against them was satisfying, not least because it was my best goal yet. I remember David White was chasing a big punt upfield and got a touch that came my way. I loved taking shots early and I was thinking, 'You know what? I'm going to have a punt here,' so as the ball came down, I hit it on an angle from 25 yards across Neville Southall and into the far corner. It was a sweet hit and the fact it was against a team of top jockeys made it even more enjoyable. We lost 3-1 but it was a good memory for me and one that I would be reminded of many years later by a surgeon who was present that day.

The next game was Watford and I tried out the new boots that Nike had sent me – a pair with green and yellow markings. I remember having a half chance but I slipped as I took the shot and it came to nothing. We drew 0-0 and on the way home, my dad said, 'What the bloody hell were those you had on your feet?'

I told him they were Nike boots and he said, 'Nike? You want to get them off your feet. Nike make trainers, not football boots.' I think it's fair to say he got that one wrong given what happened in the years that followed! I still ditched them and never wore them again, though.

On a Tuesday night, I went to watch one of my dad's teams play near The Cliff, Manchester United's training ground. He was coaching Bolton Lads' under-16s and they had a game where United's scouts could watch the lads against a team of their apprentices, to see if there were any players they wanted to take. After the game, I was stood with a few of the parents back at The Cliff and I heard my name mentioned close by, but took no notice. Then a United apprentice came up to me and said, 'Are you Paul Moulden? My gaffer wants to speak with you.'

I said, 'Your gaffer?' He said yes, so I went upstairs at The Cliff and was shown to Alex Ferguson's office. I sat down and he said, 'How's it going over at City?'

I told him it was OK, and he smiled and said, 'Good lad. I just wanted you to know I'm watching.' That was all he said and then he left. It was a compliment and I'd be lying if I said it didn't give me a lift to know people like that were keeping tabs on me, but I'd have never swapped City for United.

Back at City, we were in decline and the goals dried up for me, too, but the first home game of the new year against Oxford United would see me back in the physio room – this time with a broken back.

I was backing into the Oxford half as a goal kick came towards me and Billy Whitehurst – a thug of a footballer – must have run from ten yards behind me and smashed into my back with his knee.

It felt like he'd tried to snap me in half. He'd broken one of the wings off my vertebrae and I was lucky he hadn't cracked my spine. I was disappointed there was little or no reaction from my team-mates because nobody said jack shit to him, probably because of his reputation.

Glyn Pardoe took me to the Manchester Royal Infirmary where I sat in A&E waiting for an X-ray. There was a drunk Irish guy there as well and he started talking to us, saying we were dressed up like we played for Manchester City. 'Imagine that?' he said. 'Dressing like you play for City.' He kept chunnering on until Glyn lost it and said, 'Look pal, why don't you just sit down and shut up.' That was the end of that but me and Glyn did laugh along with the rest of A&E.

There was nothing I could do about the injury except rest while it slowly healed, and it would be seven weeks before I returned to playing.

We were trying to get out of a rut, but we were heading towards relegation and that was confirmed on the final day with a 2-0 defeat away to West Ham United. We were down, relegated for the second time in four years, and things looked bleak for the club. My season wasn't quite over yet, though. I'd been called up for England's under-19s for a tour of South America.

We flew out on 2 June and, when we arrived, Bobby Robson, the senior team manager, turned up to take the players, which was a bit of a surprise but it was a great chance for us to impress him and get into his thinking as he was clearly looking at who was coming through. I think we played Brazil twice and Uruguay twice – the Uruguayan games were diabolical because the pitches were so bad. It was like playing on a park pitch.

Halfway through the tour, we went up to see the Christ the Redeemer monument above São Paulo and we were having pictures taken and enjoying the view when Robson came over for a quiet word.

'What are you doing to try and get a bit quicker?' he asked.

I felt I was doing OK and didn't feel I was slow, but all the injuries had probably started to take a bit of zip out of my game. So I told him I was training with the Brightwells and working my nuts off, and he just said, 'OK, keep doing that. Unless you get a bit quicker, I can't see you progressing with the England squad.'

I felt it was a bit of an odd conversation to have with a 19-year-old kid. I thought if he had issues, maybe it was better just not to pick me next time, but I'd done ever so well for England at every level, so I was a bit pissed off. I might not have been David White (who was?), but what I did, I did well, and if I'm honest, I couldn't catch my breath! It didn't make me feel good, but I had to crack on.

It was the last time I was picked for my country at any level.

12

Career Interrupted

JIMMY FRIZZELL stood down as team manager in the summer of 1987, but carried on in the management team, although I can't recall how I first heard about this. I didn't know a dicky bird about his replacement Mel Machin, who had arrived from Norwich City – none of us did. I also had no idea just how detrimental to my City career Machin would be.

There is a beginning, middle and end to the story of Mel Machin and me and, though there were one or two purple patches, it mostly started badly and ended terribly.

I turned up for pre-season looking to do what I did – score goals – and get back in a good rhythm for the 1987/88 season and also carry on working towards establishing myself in the first team. We were looking to push for promotion at the first attempt.

I hadn't scored the goals I'd wanted to in the second half of the previous season, partly because I'd had a broken back that kept me out for a while. I also had competition for a starting place. Paul Stewart had been signed for £200,000 from Blackpool the previous March, plus Imre Varadi and Trevor Morley were at City, and Tony Adcock had been signed from Colchester for about £75,000. Darren Beckford had been sold for peanuts – about £15,000 to Port Vale – and I wasn't sure what direction the club was heading in.

I was wondering what my worth was because as soon as I saw Adcock in training I was like, 'Fuck me, is he supposed to be better than me; if he is, I'll show my arse in St Anne's Square!' But football is all about opinions and I had to prove my worth and show the new manager what I could do.

But I couldn't help but be worried about some of the decisions that were being made. Eric Nixon, Clive Wilson – who was a superb lad – Paul Warhurst, the Beckfords and Kenny Clements were all gone or going, and it felt like a completely different set-up that was being created.

I had no idea if Machin knew anything about me, whether he had any preconceptions or if he was going to give me a chance, so we went into pre-season with a blank sheet of paper as far as I was concerned.

But I got the impression that – for reasons known only to him – he took an instant dislike to me. I remember we were having a run down by the university playing fields, which included a track down by the River Mersey where we crossed into Sale Water Park, ran around the lake and then headed back up the other side of the river to where we'd started at the university. There was no way you could cheat other than swimming across the Mersey and coming back wet through – there was literally no other way to cut corners. Ian Brightwell and I started off by leapfrogging the stile at the beginning because there was a jam of bodies waiting to get over, and Neil McNab looked over at us and said, 'What's that all about?' but we were fit athletes and just wanted to get out clear and set off, returning in 27 minutes because we were proper fit lads.

Tony Book, Roy Bailey and Machin were all waiting at the finish line and Machin just said to us, 'Where have you two been? You must have cheated.' Roy said, 'Do you not know who he is?', looking at Brighty who, of course, had Olympians as parents. Then he looked at me and said, 'And he's as fit as he is. They've not cheated. They're always first back.' Machin said, 'Nah, they must have cheated, I'm not having that.'

The run was taking most lads 40 to 45 minutes and last in was Andy Dibble, about 30 minutes later, wet through after swimming the river, claiming he'd got lost!

Machin was adamant, despite Roy – who had done the run many times and knew the score – insisting we hadn't. 'Get them doing doggies,' Machin said, meaning we had to do extra running while we waited for the others. Roy took us around the back, put a few cones down and said not to worry. 'He's pissing in the wind, here,' he said.

Machin had some strange ways about him as a man and as a coach. There was one session where your right foot had one name – something like Bob – and your left had another, but it was nonsense, and I couldn't grasp it. I was a footballer who went out and played and stuck the ball in the back of the net when I had the chance, but Machin was on my case continually because not only did I not understand what he was on about, I thought it was a ridiculous drill.

I just felt he was on my back from day one, whereas you could see he loved Hinchy (Andy Hinchcliffe), David White and Lakey but he wasn't having me. I think it was personal and the die had been cast from that first run around Sale Water Park. Was it really down to that? Him calling me a cheat and me saying that I'd never cheated in my life. I think that is the only logical explanation and if it is, what a poor way to man-manage and get the best from your players.

We flew out to Sweden for a training camp, and I wasn't really involved in the friendlies we had against the bigger teams – just bit parts in a couple of matches against the crap sides nobody had heard of. But I was surprised to be selected for the second to last games of the tour when we were playing one of the stronger teams. In the sparse crowd, I noticed Eric Harrison; the revered talent spotter and youth-team coach from Manchester United had come along to watch the game, or had he come to watch me?

Bearing in mind the chat I'd had with Alex Ferguson a few months earlier, it seemed a long way to come and watch Manchester City's reserve team playing a game of no consequence out in the wilds of Sweden. If they were about to put an offer in or not, I'll never know, but nothing would ever come of it.

So the lads who'd played most of the games in Sweden trained on a Thursday and those who didn't trained on the Friday. That meant a few one-on-one sessions for about seven or eight of us and I ended up with Earl Barrett in mine. It meant taking on your opponent and trying to get the better of them, and we were both keen as mustard – good mates, but very competitive with no quarters asked, no quarters given.

I was never going to beat Earl on pace, but I got half a yard on him with a smart turn and started to go past him when he attempted a tackle that saw his knee go into the side of my shin. It was no more than a training ground accident and nothing malicious. I came off the pitch where Roy Bailey took a look and then disappeared to find a bag of ice. That was that, and the next day we flew back to Manchester ready for a friendly that had been organised for the first team. It was with a mixture of the reserves and A team away to Chester.

I started the game but didn't feel that comfortable. Something was niggling away around my shin, but I was thinking to myself, 'Come on, you soft arse – get on with it.' But something was wrong. The game began, I received the ball on the right flank, knocked it past my marker and ran on, but he recovered and came in from the side and behind – again, nothing malicious – but it left me with a twisted knee, ligament damage and the diagnosis would be a further six weeks on the sidelines which was really bad timing for me.

I'd been here before, so I knew it was about being patient and not getting frustrated about the situation. I rested, did strengthening exercises and physio and, after six weeks, I was able to do movement and stretches aimed at opening my knee up a bit to regain my flexibility. The rule of thumb was that once that felt good, it was time to start some gentle running, which I did.

But there was still something wrong. I couldn't get on my toes, and I was really flat-footed. My right shin was sore, and everyone was scratching their heads trying to figure out what the issue was. At the end of October, I went along to the *Manchester Evening News* Sports Personality of the Year awards for my exploits the season before. Bryan Robson, Brian McClair and loads of other top players were there and it was great to be among them and other top sports names, but I was sat there at my table with my leg in plaster because nobody knew what was wrong with it. I had a cast on for three weeks, but when I tried to run on it again, I had the same problem. I couldn't get on my toes and was flat-footed.

I had to sit in the stands watching for most of the time and, in November 1987, I watched Paul Stewart, Tony Adcock and David White all score a hat-trick as we beat Huddersfield Town 10-1 at Maine Road, trying not to feel sorry for myself while all the time wondering how many I might have scored that day. It brought it all home to me that just a year before, everything had been going tickety-boo and now I was sidelined by an injury that nobody could put a label on. Until it was sorted, I was in a weird sort of limbo, desperate to kick on and show the manager what I could do but a prisoner to my unexplained calf or shin problem. I remembered when I had been 15 and 16 and it had been touch or go whether I even carried on after my third broken leg, and then how I'd become a massive part of the first team to now back wondering where everything was heading again while others were in the team and doing really well. They were dark times for me, I have to admit.

I went to see a series of specialists, none of whom could figure out the problem, and even went to Lilleshall to see the England physios and they didn't have a clue, by which time I was approaching my wits' end. I was sent for a radioactive bone scan, but the radiographer said she couldn't find anything.

On my way out, I passed a woman who had X-rayed me in the recent past. I said hello and chatted idly for a moment, and she could probably see the look of hopelessness – or, more likely, 'Will somebody find out what the hell this is?' – in my eyes as I explained my latest fruitless examination. She told me to hang fire and not to leave just yet. She went and got a foot plate to place behind my shin where the pain and discomfort was coming from and took another X-ray with the plate under and, finally, a hairline fracture of my shin showed up. Halle-fucking-lujah.

At the weekend, the doctor usually had a round-up of injuries and ailments to assess but Dr Luft, the club doctor, was away and another guy strode in with Sherlock Holmes pants on, big brown brogues, coloured socks, short pants cut just below his knee and a tweed jacket. It was matchday and I just thought, 'What the actual fuck?'

So it was quarter to two and not that long before kick-off by the time he'd finished with the first team. I was sat in with the coaches and a few other lads who were younger than me and the doctor shouted, 'Paul Moulden!' I slumped down on my seat and Skip said, 'What are you doing? Go and see him.'

I'd been here, there and everywhere and didn't have any confidence in this guy. I sighed and said, 'Where have they got this clown from?' Skip told me to go and see him, and but for him I wouldn't have bothered, but it turned out to be another massive life lesson for me. I went through and sat down, and he introduced himself as a former doctor with the Marines, then asked what my problem was. I explained what had gone on over the past few months and he asked if it hurt when he pressed on a certain part of my shin. Did it ever!

I told him I had a hairline fracture that had just been identified, but I couldn't do anything about it until the club doctor came back. He said, 'That's not your problem, son. The issue is you've been tying your bootlaces too tight on your calf and your calf has bled. You've done nothing for a day afterwards and even worse, you've then flown in a plane and what's happened is your calf muscle has stuck to your shin.' It turned out that this was quite a common problem that he'd seen in Marines who tied their boots too tight round their calves on long marches carrying heavy kit. In fact, I hadn't fastened laces too tight round my calf, but it turned out that the blow to my shin and calf had manifested itself in the same way and that's why he recognised it immediately.

I said, 'OK then, what needs to be done?'

He told me it was a simple nick, and that the hairline issue would have already been and gone, so I was booked in for surgery and on 20 December Mr Markham operated to rectify the problem – another great Christmas!

I'd gone from pre-season and missed the next five months while people tried to find out what the issue was, and this guy, who I'd thought was a clown to begin with, had identified the problem in minutes. I often wonder what would've happened had I not got off my chair to see this remarkable doctor.

Within three weeks, I was playing again. My first game for Mel Machin was in January 1988 – an FA Cup third round tie away to Huddersfield Town and, all of a sudden, he was my best mate. Brighty had put us 1-0 up after about five minutes and there must have been nearly 10,000 City fans at Leeds Road that afternoon. Bear in mind we'd beaten them 10-1 at Maine Road in the league just a couple of months before – they scored twice just after the break to lead 2-1. I came on as sub and Machin was complaining about something or other and the referee went across to talk with him. He must have carried on complaining because the ref then sent him off.

We were seven minutes into added time when John Gidman's free kick made it 2-2 and won us a replay, but Machin was in hot water with the FA. A few days later, he was summoned to a disciplinary hearing in Manchester, and I had to go as a witness with a team-mate, while Jimmy Frizzell and Machin sat in the front. On the way to town, he was saying, 'This is what happened, isn't it boys?' He was instructing us on what to say at the hearing.

It didn't sit well with me, but we went into the enquiry, said what we'd been told and then a guy from the FA said,

'Thank you very much Mr Moulden for coming in,' and as I got up to leave, I passed the referee and linesmen who had brought the complaint and they had been sat there listening to me tell lies behind the door. I wasn't happy with any of it, and I told myself I'd never put myself in that position again. Machin was fined, but it further soured our relationship, only this time from my side. He'd called me a cheat and made me look a liar in front of an FA panel, so there was only one way our relationship was going to go from that point on. I hinted as much on the car journey back to Maine Road and Machin said nothing in response.

At least I was back in training and starting to feel much sharper so, when I scored against Plymouth Argyle not long after, it felt like a massive weight had been lifted because that was my first goal in ten months, which felt like an age.

I was getting the odd game here and there, but it was always because there was nobody else he could call on due to injuries and/or suspensions. If Jimmy Rous, the caretaker, had remembered his boots on a Saturday, I think he'd have got a game ahead of me.

So, I ended that season with one full appearance, eight off the bench and one goal. In fact, by the time 1988/89 started, I had played a handful of games and scored twice in 21 months. Things had to change for me and, as far as Machin was concerned, I'd had my fill. If he didn't want me,

I'd go somewhere else and I'd make sure he knew how pissed off I was.

It was the last thing I wanted, but my head was all over the place and it looked like my time at City was coming to a sorry conclusion.

Then something else happened that had me questioning where I stood in Machin's plans. Every year before the season began, we put on the new kit for the team photo, so we gathered at Maine Road and John Peters, the club photographer, got everyone on his list to line up with a front, back and middle row, only my name wasn't down. While all the other lads got changed, I just sat there like a spare part. They went out and John told Skip the picture looked lopsided, and we needed another player. Skip came in, gave me the kit, and told me to go out and join the others for the photograph. Privately, John had told me he was going to get me on somehow and he'd been as good as his word.

13

Dead Man Walking?

BRIAN GAYLE had joined City from Wimbledon during the close season and what a top bloke he was. In training he was superb, but in our first two league games of 1988/89 he had a nightmare. It was like he was two different animals, but he got there as time went on.

I wasn't anywhere near the first team in pre-season, so when the lads lost at Hull on the opening day I had detached myself from feeling part of everything and, if I'm honest, I couldn't have cared less.

Wayne Biggins was up front, confidence in the team was low and in the second game, Oldham Athletic – the team Jimmy Frizzell had labelled 'a bunch of yard dogs' a few years back – came to haunt us and they beat us 4-1 at Maine Road. All of a sudden Mel Machin was under fantastic pressure, and I was hoping they'd get shut if the truth be told.

I'd won the FA Youth Cup, Lancashire League, Central League, and I had been scoring goals for the club I loved and now Machin had taken it all away from me, and for what exactly? This was my own back yard, where I'd grown up, and I just thought to myself, 'This cannot happen.' I felt strong, I felt fit, and I'd had enough.

To rub salt in the wound, we had a reserves against first team game at the end of pre-season and I wasn't even in that! I decided I'd had enough and was ready to jack it all in. I wasn't going in for training anymore, and instead I would start looking for a job on civvy street and I was more than prepared to walk away from football for good.

After a couple of days, Skip called me to find out where I was, and I told him I'd sacked it off and I wouldn't be coming back. I'd been up to my dad's work and spoken to the foreman who said he'd find me a job and I was genuinely prepared to start a life away from football. My head had gone completely. Skip said there was a game on Wednesday afternoon and to come in beforehand and have a chat, which I agreed to do out of respect for him. He told me that if it didn't happen at City, it would somewhere else and that I needed to stay fit and visible.

I could see he had my best interests at heart as he always had, and what he said made sense – why throw it all away because of Machin who, in my opinion, was a cock at the best of times? So I went in on Thursday and Roy Bailey, taking the piss, asked if I was feeling better now. He then told me I'd been through worse and to keep my chin up and keep going. I felt that everyone except Machin had belief in me and I took strength from that instead of wallowing in my own frustration. It put an end to the 'nobody wants me, and nobody likes me' feeling I'd had, and I threw myself back into training with a different mindset – albeit one that still wasn't going to put up with any shit from Machin.

We did a Tony Book running session on the Friday – and he ran the legs off you in those sessions because if you didn't have a game over the weekend, he classed that as a two-day holiday! After that, I got changed and was heading out when Machin called me into the coach's office. I went in and he said, 'There's a rumour going around this football club that you're a goalscorer.'

I looked at him and said, 'Who's spreading vicious rumours then?'

Skip was behind him, and his face dropped, so I decided to rein myself in before I got yet another verbal lashing. I said, 'Yeah, I've been known to score once or twice.'

Machin said, 'Well, you're starting tomorrow.'

I thought, 'Fuck me – set me up to fail, or what?' I'd just finished a mammoth running session and now I'd be playing away to Leeds United the next day. Don't get me wrong, it was very much mixed emotions. I would be playing up front for Manchester City at Elland Road which was everything I wanted – it was just that, at that moment, my legs felt dead, and it didn't feel I would be getting a fair crack of the whip. But I'd give it a go.

As it was, I went out and played really well. I didn't score, but we drew 1-1 to get us off the bottom of the Second Division. After the game, my dad said that if I could play like that after the session I'd had the day before, I just needed the rub of the green and I'd be away. He said I needed to get a few games under my belt to see what I could do.

The following Saturday we were home to Brighton, and I kept my place in the starting XI. It was strange running out at Maine Road given all the various scenarios I'd played out in my head over the past 18 months, and it felt like I'd never been there before – I can't explain it better than that – but I'd been through so much and everything felt different. We were wearing blue shirts and white shorts – my favourite City kit and one that we hadn't worn for a while (though I had in the reserves). I didn't like the all-blue kit.

I felt like I was seeing everything through new eyes. I looked around before kick-off and just thought, 'You're in your own back yard, you've scored goals and played well here and no one is going to stop you now after all you've been through. So, get your arse into gear, you've got a chance.' That was all I ever wanted, a chance. It was a tight game, and I played a poor pass in to Trevor Morley, but he did brilliantly, turning and putting Brighty through to score. I knew I was playing catch-up with my team-mates but my boots didn't feel right, so at half-time I changed them for a pair of Umbro Internationals, and they felt really good. I was focused on what I needed to do. I had to score, because if I didn't then I knew I'd be back out again.

If I got the opportunity, I was going to shoot on sight. We went back out and I received a pass, turned my marker and was just about within shooting distance, so I went on to autopilot, trusted my instincts, and hit a shot from 35 yards that flew into the top-right corner like an arrow. It was one of the best feelings in my life. All the doubt, being called a cheat, the doom and gloom and frustration was gone in an instant and I felt I'd proved what I was capable of, if to nobody else, to myself, that I could still do it. I felt I was back, and I still had a future at City whether Machin was in charge or not.

Three days later we were away to Chelsea, and I was getting on the coach for our legend of a driver to take us south. Derek Sutton was a massive part of everything the first-team squad did in those days – he was a big, middle-aged guy who was larger than life in every respect. He had the ear of the players because we knew he had been there, seen it and done it over the years as City's driver. He also drove the reserves and youth team and he'd seen managers come and go, as well as players and staff, and if Derek told you to do something, invariably you did it or he'd leather you with an Eric Nixon-style rough-up. He didn't take any crap and he always told you straight whether you were a wet-behind-the-ears youth-team player or club captain. The younger players took notice when he spoke, and one thing he never did was give praise away cheaply. But underneath all the tough outer layers, cliché or not, he had a heart of gold and was totally dependable and trustworthy.

As I climbed on the coach, he said, 'Fucking hell, Mouldy. Great goal on Saturday. Welcome back to the big time.'

It was high praise indeed and the 'big time' with Derek meant the first team. I bounded on to the coach and was momentarily lost in thought when I drew level with Machin who said, 'I've watched that goal you scored against Brighton and the keeper got a fingertip to it.'

I looked at him, half wondering if he was serious – which he was – and said, 'Good job it wasn't a fucking hand then, wasn't it?'

He'd been on his arse, we'd lost the opening two games and drawn the next and I'd scored one and played a part in another to get that first win and he'd managed to find a negative in one of the best goals I'd ever scored. 'Fuck right off' was my first thought. I couldn't believe what had come out of his mouth and, as I sat down, I happened to catch Derek's eyes in the huge rear-view mirror at the front and he didn't have to move his head or say a thing – his eyes were telling me what he thought of Machin's management style, which in my case was do anything and everything to stop me feeling positive or good about myself. I wondered if my pals Paul Merson and Micky Thomas were getting the same treatment at Arsenal.

I got off the bus at the hotel that we were staying at in Beaconsfield and, as I got my bag, Derek said, 'Fucking hell, from a man who is going to lose his job soon that was some comment wasn't it?'

I said, 'Derek, I couldn't believe it. What's his fucking problem?' He replied, 'Mouldy, you just crack on lad. Don't ever lose belief in your ability.' It was probably the first time in the six years I'd known Derek that he'd been totally serious with me and, because he'd said it, it really meant something to me.

At Stamford Bridge, I scored again as we beat Chelsea 3-1. I held my run and as a long ball was knocked down and because I'd played back-to-back games and my legs had almost gone, I thought I'd take it early and I smashed it over the keeper and into the roof of the net from about 25 yards out. I had a great game, I'd been involved in all the goals, and I'd scored in successive matches, so it felt like happy days again.

We followed that up with wins over Barnsley and Blackburn as well as beating Plymouth Argyle in the League Cup to make it five wins on the bounce and six without a defeat, so from being maybe one or two games away from the sack, Machin had probably thought he had nothing to lose by throwing me in. I'm not saying it was all down to me, far from it, but we were now the Second Division form team going into our home match against Portsmouth.

I went into that game with a broken nose sustained four days earlier when Colin Hendry had back-heeled me in the beak. There was blood everywhere, but I carried on playing and had it stitched up afterwards. Dr Luft had put stitches in, and I could see one in front of my eye that looked like a climbing rope going up Everest. Roy Bailey told me I'd have to have my nose reset on the Monday, which he did, and on the Tuesday morning he asked me how I was feeling for the Pompey game. I told him I was fine – I was better than fine, in fact.

I went out and warmed up and, as I was walking off, Graeme Hogg came over and said, 'All right Paul, how are you doing?'

'I didn't know you were playing for these,' I said. I knew Graeme from his days at United and youth and reserve-team matches, and he always seemed like a decent sort. The game started and I was like a busy bee, here, there and everywhere and I remember going up for a header with Hogg and, as we jumped up, his hand came around my face and he put two fingers up my nostrils and fuck me, the pain was unbearable. I can smile now, but Jesus it was agony and it just showed that desire you needed to get the better of whoever you were up against; in 90 minutes of football you only had enemies.

Still, I played on, scored again and we won 4-1, so it didn't knock me off my stride, even though it makes my eyes water now to just think of the incident.

Despite all the goals and victories, I still felt like I needed to score every game to keep my place because I always had that feeling that, given the opportunity, Machin would find a reason to drop me. We were winning games with the odd blip here and there. I bagged another in the League Cup second leg away to Plymouth – a 6-3 win at Home Park – then we beat them in the league four days later, 1-0, and again at their place, to keep us on the shoulders of the top three.

We lost 1-0 at Ipswich, drew 0-0 with Birmingham and then lost 1-0 at West Brom. In and around those games with Plymouth, I half expected the axe after each one, but I was surprised to see my name in the starting XI after our loss at The Hawthorns for the League Cup tie against Sheffield United at Maine Road.

As a kid, I used to watch some of the great players play at Maine Road. I used to study Peter Barnes and Dennis

Tueart and every small detail about their game and their playing styles. I knew everything about that pitch, from the goal markings to the sidelines and corner triangles. I'd absorbed it all.

Now, it was me playing in front of the City fans. For every home game, at 13 minutes to three – 13 was my lucky number – I'd go into the gym for five minutes or so in my kit and match boots and just practise shooting on the AstroTurf or whatever the carpeted floor was. I'd get some clean strikes in and just get in the mood and, that day, I was in the zone, but even though I would take the match ball home later that evening, the highlight for me was when I span and played a through ball to Lakey who went through and tucked it home. It was probably one of the best goals seen at Maine Road for a few years and when I came off at the end, it was Lakey's goal and my part in it that I was thinking of and little else, not the three goals I'd scored. I so wanted to be recognised as a good footballer as well as a goalscorer. We won 4-2 and I hadn't realised it was my 50th game for City, so it was a nice way to mark that landmark – but I only really wanted to see Lakey's goal on TV later that night.

The goals were flying in, I was making them for my team-mates, and I was on cloud nine – what could possibly go wrong?

14

Why Always Me?

I WAS going to do everything I could to keep my place and force Mel Machin's hand, so there was a bit of 'go on then, drop me now' about me during that period. I'd scored seven goals in the 13 games I'd played in since being recalled, which was a decent enough return, but I never once felt I was guaranteed a start at any stage.

Some people might think that's a good way to keep you on your toes, but it can also result in you trying too hard, snatching at chances, and playing with too much urgency.

It wasn't that I was playing badly, just it was always at the back of my mind that Machin still didn't rate me, and I felt he was always looking for that opportunity to leave me out. Sure enough, around late October and during November, I was back to square one and out of the side for no obvious reason.

I remember Rob McCaffrey from Granada TV contacting me to do an interview at Hacken Lane for *Kick Off* – the regional football show that aired on a Friday evening. It was partly about my world records as a kid, but I think he had an inkling that I was pissed off, because it was mostly about me being last season's top scorer – but being in and out of the team this season.

I was open and honest when he asked me why I wasn't a regular starter given my goals record. 'I haven't got a clue,' I said, and then it just all came out as I proceeded to dig out Machin in everything but name. I actually held back a lot, because I could have slaughtered him that day, and maybe I should have.

I'd scored 11 in 24 games that season, but I would have loved to have had a long run in the side, got my feet under the table and felt settled and happy because I honestly thought there was no stopping me.

Forget Mario Balotelli because that T-shirt with 'Why always me?' on it should have been worn by me back in 1988/89. If anything went wrong, it was down to me. It felt like whenever anyone was fit or I didn't score then I was out, and in late December I found myself back in the reserves for a derby against United at Old Trafford.

Former Nottingham Forest, England and Norwich striker Justin Fashanu had been signed on a short-term contract while Machin had a look at him and there was a decent enough crowd in for the 'mini-derby' as they called it. In fairness, it turned out to be some game, but I also learned about the character and integrity of Justin that night. What a lovely guy.

It was Fash who put us in front, sending a thumping header home from Michael Hughes's cross, but we conceded twice before half-time to go in 2-1 down. Machin stormed into the dressing room and, surprise, surprise, started tearing a strip off me. What a fucking shocker, right?

But Fash wasn't having it. 'Nah, you're out of order,' he told Machin. 'If I could have played up front with anybody in my career, it'd be him. He works hard, never stops running or finding space and he's always looking to play people in.'

Machin said nothing and stormed out of the dressing room, but I suddenly felt eight feet tall as nobody had ever really had my back like that before, especially when I was getting a bollocking. It was strange and even Skip didn't say anything – it was just a really odd atmosphere. Let's not forget, Fash had been one of the first million-pound strikers in England and had done enough for Brian Clough to make him one of Forest's record signings, but here he was, standing up for me, which meant a hell of a lot to me.

We went back out and went 3-1 down soon after, but we were playing really well. We were actually battering them, but with 86 minutes played we were still a couple of goals behind until Trevor Morley – who I was really close to and was another fantastic guy – pulled one back. Then the grandstand finish. On 89, I tucked the ball home to make it 3-3 and 90 seconds later, I scored again to make it 4-3. The City fans were going mad, and I'll always remember Piccadilly Radio put out the final score on their sports round-up later as a 3-1 win for United, not realising (or checking) we'd scored three in the last four minutes. Fash was class that evening, as a man as well as a footballer.

On Boxing Day, a couple of weeks later, we travelled to Stoke, and the City fans had decided it was going to be a fancy dress day out. Jesus, we must have had 12,000 fans at the Victoria Ground that day and it was absolutely unbelievable. We travelled down on the coach, seeing every type of inflatable you can imagine in the cars and coaches that passed. It was fantastic to see, and it geed you up because, with support like that, you wanted to go out and give them a good show.

I'd played the previous game, so I was expecting to feature in this one and, when we arrived, everywhere in our dressing room was wet through so Roy Bailey and Derek Sutton used a tub of old towels we took with us to dry the benches, walls and floor. It was a tactic to put you off and I'd been party to something similar at Maine Road once under Billy McNeill against Watford when we'd been told that John Barnes didn't like the cold. So McNeill told all the apprentices to take all the fuses out of the heaters and wet the benches. It was a bit of a myth judging by Barnes's performance in that game, but I digress.

I offered to help Roy and Derek, as did Brighty and David White, because they were family to us and we honestly didn't mind, but with Roy's behaviour I had an inkling that I was in for some bad news. Ahead of the game we were all gathered as Machin delivered the team to play Stoke. He started by saying, 'Right, we're going to change formation today,' and I just laughed out loud and said, 'Fuck off. That means I'm not playing, doesn't it?'

Roy said, 'Shut up, Mouldy,' but I looked at Machin and said, 'OK, then, am I playing?'

Machin said, 'Well, we're changing things around today,' and I just cut him off and said, 'You're an absolute fucking joke, pal.'

Roy was trying to calm me down and Machin looked at me and said, 'Right, you're fined two weeks' wages, Paul's not playing.'

Machin left the room and Roy tried to stop me following him, but I slipped past him and caught up with Machin who I'd had a bellyful of by that stage. I said, 'Are you taking the fucking piss or what?'

He said, 'Well, we don't think your game is suited to this formation,' and I said, 'Stoke are piss poor, what are you fucking on about? Not suited?' I was 21 years old at this time, but I'd grown up ten years in a short space of time.

Nobody in that dressing room was left in any doubt that day whatsoever about my thoughts on Mel Machin and whether I'd burned any bridges or not; I didn't know or care. But I felt good telling him what I thought. As it turned out, Stoke battered us 3-1. I had a mate among the City fans who took the inflatable Frankenstein to games and was at Stoke that day. He said that as soon as it was announced I wasn't in the starting XI, he and those around him were saying we wouldn't win. He added, it wasn't because I was that good – thanks Kev (and neither was your plastering!) – but it just upset the team by changing things around. My head had gone that day and I paid little attention to what went on if I'm totally honest. Apart from the result, the manager seemed to be in self-destruct mode and hell-bent on taking the team down with him.

I just couldn't understand it. If you have a goalscorer in your team, they can be like gold dust. For any coach, it should be a relief to have a player who can score the goals, snatch a victory or a draw. While it's not about individuals and it's all for the team, the bottom line is that player is on the score sheet regularly for a reason and that is because you're winning games. But there was none of that with Machin. Figuring him out was like trying to solve a Rubik's Cube.

John Deehan was Machin's assistant manager – another lovely bloke who I had the utmost respect for – but even he didn't have an answer for why I was being treated the way I was. He just told me to keep my head down and keep working hard, which was probably all he could say in the circumstances.

But it was continually gnawing away at me.

I was also out of contract in the summer and, as we started 1989, I arranged a meeting with Jimmy Frizzell to talk about the possibility of a new deal.

I went in and sat down at his desk, and he asked where my dad was. I asked why I needed my dad, and more to the point, where was Machin? 'He won't be coming,' Jimmy said, and I suppose I shouldn't have expected anything less.

I had been chatting with Trevor Morley, who told me he was on £750 a week and had been given a £50,000 signing-on fee, so I told Jimmy I wanted parity with Trevor.

He sort of half laughed and said, 'That's not going to happen, Paul.' Instead, the club were offering me a two-year extension and increasing my wage from £350 to £400.

'What about a signing-on fee?'

'There's no signing-on fee, Paul – that's it.'

I told him I wouldn't be signing the contract.

I started the new year in and out of the team and in late January, after I'd scored in a 4-1 win over Hull City, I picked up a muscle strain that kept me out for four weeks, and after an injection I was back in training in mid-February. That gave Machin another excuse to keep me on the bench, but when I came on and got the goal that earned us a 1-1 draw at West Brom to keep us second, the pressure was on Machin to play me again – but he resisted, and I was 12th man again for the 1-0 defeat at Watford in the game that followed.

Then, I was named in the starting XI against Leicester City, but what an awful day that proved to be when Lakey went up for a header, clashed with a Leicester player and then dropped on the ground with his legs twitching. It turned out he'd swallowed his tongue and, for a moment, we thought we were going to lose him right there on the Maine Road turf. It took an age for the doctor to get out to him and there was an air of panic on and off the pitch before he finally made it out and they managed to get him breathing again. It's rotten enough seeing someone go off with a bad injury, never mind witnessing a freak accident. None of us really had the stomach for the game after that and, though we won 4-2, the only real high that day was going into the dressing room and seeing Lakey sat there as happy as Larry. What a relief that was.

My contract 'negotiations' continued to be a source of amusement for me. Having turned down the club's paltry £50-per-week rise, I was invited to see Jimmy Frizzell again, who informed me the offer was now £100 per week – with no signing-on fee. I told Jimmy I wasn't signing it.

I was benched again for the next game against Chelsea – I think it was live on ITV – and I sat there watching my old mate Clive Wilson, who was outstanding that day, and just thinking what a poor policy City had at the time, paying money to bring players in who weren't as good as the ones who had been homegrown and cost nothing – with Clive being a prime example. He could have served City fantastically well for ten years, as he did Chelsea, Spurs and QPR. Earl Barrett, Paul Warhurst, Darren Beckford, Eric Nixon, Paul Simpson, John Beresford and Clive – all sold for peanuts or even given away.

Machin played the left-footed Gerry Taggart at right-back that day, and we got murdered, though the 3-2 loss suggests it was closer than it actually was. It wasn't Gerry's fault, but couldn't John Beresford or Earl have slotted in there instead had they still been at the club, or maybe even Andy Hinchcliffe could have swapped flanks and Gerry play on the left? Machin's thinking left me scratching my head at the best of times.

A week later, I was back in for our game away to Walsall, and you can get a sense of me not knowing what was coming next. Machin's signings always came first, so it was usually only if one of them was missing or unfit that I'd get a look in. Dean Smith – future Villa and Norwich boss – was playing that day but I think we went 2-0 down before we scored on 44,

45 and then 46 minutes to lead 3-2 and I got a couple of them. Andy Dibble's groin went, and Nigel Gleghorn had to go in goal before David Oldfield gave Walsall a late chance with a bad mistake and it ended 3-3, which was enough to keep us second in the table, but the game had felt like a calamity from start to finish.

I started five of the next seven matches, but the one I didn't away to Blackburn left Machin in no doubt as to what the City fans thought of me being on the bench. It was a red-hot day at Ewood Park, and Roy Bailey put the manager's bench against the fence just in front of where the City fans were housed. I'd played well the week before in the 2-1 win over Swindon but here I was, dropped again, and when I came out, City fans behind were coming up and asking me, 'Why aren't you playing, Paul?' I just said, 'I haven't a clue,' and when Machin came out, the City fans were giving him pelters, proper lifelong Blues and no-nonsense Mancs and some of them let's just say, were blunt speakers, with the gist being, 'Why the fuck is he not playing?' Machin got slaughtered that day and I actually felt sorry for him, it was that bad. Afterwards – and after we'd been dicked 4-0 – Roy got a major bollocking.

'Who put that fucking bench there?' Machin asked. Roy said, 'Me, it was cold in the dugout, and it was a nice day.' He'd meant well, but he'd unwittingly thrown Machin to the dogs that day.

I knew that was also the end for me at City, because whether he said it or not, he'd hold me accountable for what had happened.

It was around this time that I first became aware of a rumour about me that I honestly had no idea about. There was an awards ceremony I was attending so I went for a pint with my mate Mark in Didsbury beforehand.

He was a big Blue and when I sat down with the drinks, he just blurted out, 'You're not in the team because you're shagging Mel Machin's daughter, aren't you?' I almost choked on my beer. I asked him where that had come from and he said it was a massive rumour among the City fans that Machin hated me because I'd been secretly seeing his daughter – so much so, it was accepted as fact.

There's been a few things in my life that I've never properly had the chance to address, and this is one of them, but I can categorically say that not only is it not true, but I also don't even know if Machin has a daughter! If he does, I've never met her, nor at the time was I aware of her existence. People say there's no smoke without fire, but in this case, there was definitely no smoke and certainly no fire. It was probably something somebody had assumed and put out there, but it became a myth that I still get asked about today. As far as I'm concerned, the fact Machin pissed me about was down to him being a shit manager and nothing to do with anything other than that.

Such was the lottery of my career at the time, I was back in the week after, but I couldn't buy a goal in the game I played, so with three matches to go I had to dig deep and find one from somewhere. I played against Crystal Palace, but when Andy Dibble's groin went again and Nigel Gleghorn once again took the gloves, we were happy to take a 1-1 draw, though we weren't right as a team that day with too many whinging about the heat or the pitch being too dry. It was probably just nerves. I hadn't prepared well for the game the day before either because I drove up to Lancaster to pick up someone beforehand and drove back again when I should have been resting up. However, a win against Bournemouth at Maine Road five days later would mean we would definitely go up.

I got the nod ahead of David Oldfield and I was determined that neither I nor we as a team would fuck this up. Things couldn't have started much better, with Andy Hinchcliffe's cross to Trevor Morley eventually falling to me about eight yards out and me thinking, 'How do you like these, Paul?' as I smashed it past the keeper to put us 1-0 up with just two minutes played.

Trev made it 2-0 on 39 minutes with a classy goal, and it was happy days. Then, just on half-time, I was on the edge of the box when Shaun Teale took me out with a tackle that I later discovered cracked and broke my ankle. We'd won a free kick but I wasn't going anywhere. It wasn't a bad break as such, and I could just about walk on it, so when the ref asked me if I was OK I said I was and got up ready for the free kick.

Andy Hinchcliffe took it, it beat the wall and the keeper went down low and pushed it up on to the crossbar where it dropped for me to tap into the empty net and we went in 3-0 up at half-time. Even happier days and promotion done and dusted, or so we thought. I had a bigger issue, though – I couldn't walk – but I was running on pure adrenaline, and I would have carried on playing with one leg that day, I think.

We went off at the break and Roy asked if I was OK to carry on and I said I was fine. I knew that if I gave Machin any excuse, he'd take me off and put Oldfield on, so I wasn't going to show that I was in any pain whatsoever. I ran out for the second half and the ankle was sore and a bit stiff, but we played on, I did OK and on 75 minutes I went off and was replaced by Oldfield with the score at 3-1. Bournemouth made it 3-2 soon after, but we went into added time with the crowd desperate for the ref to blow for full time – only he played another seven minutes and, with almost the last kick of the game, they won a penalty which Luther Blissett blasted home to make it 3-3. Fuck me. How had we fucked this up? It should have been a comfortable 4-0 or 5-1, yet, somehow, we'd conceded three goals and we were sick as the proverbial parrot. It meant we now needed to get a point from our final game away to Bradford City.

I had to play in that one.

By the evening my ankle was causing me a lot of pain, but I knew that if I went on Sunday to have it looked at then I wouldn't be playing against Bradford. So, instead, I went into work on Monday and just said to Roy, 'Can you have a look at this for me?' It was sort of an 'off-the-record' check – and, bear in mind Roy wanted me to be playing and no one suspected that there was a crack in my ankle, he came up with a plan. He told me to stay with him on Tuesday, Wednesday was a day off, but Thursday I would have to train because anyone with a chance of being picked needed to prove their fitness in the Thursday session and I'd need to play at least half the practice game.

I went in and asked Roy what he suggested before I played, and he said he'd strap my ankle up tight – but that's all he could do – so that's what we did and I lasted 45 minutes without showing the agony I was in to Machin and, afterwards, Roy said to rest on Friday and he'd sort it with the manager.

The day before the game, I still hadn't signed a new deal and I was invited to meet Jimmy Frizzell for a third time. I wondered whether this time the offer would be one that showed the club really believed in me and wanted me to stay.

I went into Jimmy's office trying to feel optimistic but expecting to be disappointed. The last offer had been a £100 rise – still almost half the wage Trevor Morley was on – and this was make or break as there was no time left.

Jimmy was alone again – no last-minute interjection from Machin and you know why? He didn't give a toss either way. Jimmy said, 'The offer is another £25, Paul, £425 per week and two more years.'

I just shook my head. 'Would you sign that, Jim?'

He smiled and said, 'Probably not, son.'

That was the end of my discussions for a new contract and, effectively, spelled the end of my time as a City player. But I still had a job to do – help my club win promotion and, if that could be my final contribution for my boyhood team, it wouldn't be a bad way to end my time.

Roy Bailey was as good as his word, and I was named in the starting XI for the game at Bradford. Looking back, I know I shouldn't have played – how can you give your best with a broken ankle? But Machin had made me that way. The fear of being dropped again or hauled off was always there in the back of my mind, clouding my decisions.

A chance fell my way and I hit across the keeper and wide – but the pain was ridiculous, and it was just too sore. But I wanted to help my team get promoted and, despite us going behind and still trailing 1-0 with 86 minutes played, I received the ball out left and spotted David White's run. I played into space, and he galloped on to it and sent in a low cross that

Trevor Morley slid home to make it 1-1 and get the goal that finally won us promotion to the First Division.

I could hardly walk at the end of the game, and because of the club's refusal to pay me what I felt I was worth, I knew that it was almost certainly my last appearance for City, so at least I had ended by contributing towards promotion, broken ankle or not.

Heading a ball – a very rare sight

George Lawrence, me, Shaun Brook (looking dapper as usual)

Bournemouth playing Blackburn Rovers

Scoring a hat-trick against Hull City. My old mate Peter Swan is in goal – he's usually a centre-half

What a player –
Luther Blissett

What a kit – Brighton days

Happy times

Birmingham City vs Charlton Athletic, the last game of the season. It finished off a great team effort to get the result that kept us in the league

Putting a future England manager on his backside

With Andy Saville, another great striker

Birmingham City Football Club

PAUL MOULDEN

Hear Paul talking on

0891 121188

DAILY Mirror

Trevor Morgan/ Andy Saville haircut. Three months later on. Thanks lads!

With Bobby Robson

Joe, Ted, Louie (with the scarf) – their first time at a league ground

15
Cherry-Picked

I NEVER wanted to leave Manchester City.

It was my club, my back yard and I had so many friends there on and off the pitch. I loved every minute of playing for City.

One man had taken all that away from me and as he had just taken City back to the top flight – by luck more than anything else – there was no way he was going anywhere and, as it was a case of him or me, it had to be me. I couldn't stomach another 12 months of his management and I needed to play regular football and get my career back on track again. He'd messed with my head to the point where I just couldn't do it again.

The manager had made it perfectly clear that he didn't value me and the contract 'discussions' had been a joke. I literally had no choice but to move on. My contract had expired, I was a free agent, I needed to crack on. I collected my things from Maine Road a few days after the Bradford game and, as I left, I got in my car and started crying. One bloke had taken everything away from me and that moment was the worst of my life.

Had it been my fault? Had I brought all this on myself? If I'd not been delivering when I played, I'd say that maybe I had been my own worst enemy, but it just wasn't the case.

I was a homegrown player, I was only 21, and I'd scored 26 goals from 78 appearances – 22 of those had been off the bench. They are decent enough stats for a young striker, but I always wonder what they might have been had I been given longer runs in the team – and, of course, had I not suffered a catalogue of different broken bones along the way.

I was in agony all summer and I wasn't able to do any running with Robbie Brightwell or kick a ball for six weeks.

City's chief scout Ken Barnes sent me a lovely letter saying, in as many words, that it was an absolute joke that I'd been allowed to leave, that I'd come to the club as a kid, given everything I possibly could, and he was ashamed of the way I'd been treated. I still have that letter. Tony Book told me much the same thing, which I really appreciated.

But I couldn't waste time feeling sorry for myself. I had to find somewhere else to play football. I was free to go to whichever club I wanted to and, to a certain extent, I was master of my own destiny – City were still entitled to a fee for me as it wasn't quite the Bosman era just yet.

I didn't have any representation to consult, but if I had, I'd like to think they would have given Alex Ferguson a call at United or Brian Clough at Nottingham Forest after the interest they'd shown in me.

I'd actually had a couple of dealings with Clough in my career and I knew he would have been somebody who would have got the very best out of me.

The first was when we were playing Nottingham Forest at Maine Road and I had to warm up behind the linesman, so I was sort of in front of the Forest bench. From behind, I heard the unmistakeable voice of Cloughie saying to me, 'Young man, fuck off up the other end!'

Roy Bailey was the only person to stand up for me and shouted across, 'Come on, Brian, give him a break, he's got to warm up there.'

Cloughie said, 'Well, I can't see,' and Roy suggested he should maybe stand up.

The next time I came across him was after a reserve game at Maine Road. I'd had a decent match but wasn't playing in the first team and as I walked back up the tunnel after we had finished, Cloughie was passing and asked, 'How fit are you?'

I told him I was bang on and he then said, 'How come you're not playing for the first team, here?' I told him I didn't have a clue and so he turned to Skip and said, 'Why's he not playing? Is he worth a place?'

Skip wasn't one to sing your praises to your face, but he just said I was definitely worth a place, and he didn't know why I wasn't playing either. Cloughie asked, 'Is this young man for sale? If I came in with an offer tomorrow, could I buy him?'

Skip looked at me and then looked at Cloughie and said, 'Have a go.' As Cloughie wandered off, Skip said, 'It'd be a great place to play football, wouldn't it?'

At the end of the 1987/88 season, we'd travelled to Australia. This was memorable for two reasons; firstly because I was introduced to Neil Fuller, who was a lad of my age who'd broken and later lost his leg in July 1987 playing for the Australian under-18 team. We were all so disappointed for him, it was unimaginable, but he'd had a major artery bleed that had been missed as his leg was put in plaster. Look him up, see what he accomplished! A truly amazing man. Secondly, we played in a five-a-side competition for City. Forest were also involved in it and Cloughie was all over me. I spoke with his son Nigel, and he told me his dad wanted to sign me and play me deeper as a number ten, but after we headed home I never heard anything else about it, which was a shame because I would have loved to have played for Cloughie and I would have jumped at the chance at that time because not much was happening at City.

Fast forwarding back to the end of the 1988/89 season, I'd taken my mum shopping and as we walked in with bags of groceries, the phone rang. It was Alex Ferguson, who wished me all the best and said he had no idea why City had released me. I put the phone down and I did wonder if someone was having a laugh, I couldn't believe it was him, but it was him all right, it was such a bolt out of the blue. It was a classy touch, but sadly there was no invite to go and train with United.

I also received a call from Stoke City, so I travelled down the M6 and met manager Mick Mills, who I'd always admired as a player. I had a chat with him and had a look around, but I just didn't get a good feeling for the club. I couldn't put my finger on it and even though I was only 45 minutes away from home, I decided it wasn't for me.

Then I got another call, this time from Bournemouth's managing director Brian Tiler inviting me to go down and have a look around. He was a genuinely lovely guy and I thought, 'Why not?' He told me there was no pressure and to just come, have a look and see if I got a feel for the place.

As a player, I had decent memories of playing against Bournemouth, and the previous season with City, I'd scored the winning goal in a 1-0 victory at Dean Court as well. Thinking back, that game had been quite funny, actually.

David White had crossed the ball in, and I'd gone to hit it with my right foot stretched out and my left knee underneath me, but it took a deflection and struck my left knee and flew into the net like being punched by a fist. It looked like a great finish.

Afterwards, I went into the players' lounge and a journalist came up to me and said, 'I want to speak with Paul Moulden, can you get him out for me?' I looked at him and thought, 'You what?!', but then I decided to have a bit of fun. I went back into the dressing room and primed up Brian Gayle – who, in case you've never seen him, is of mixed race, 6ft 2in with a moustache, whereas I'm white-skinned, five foot nothing, no facial hair. So, Brian went out and pretended to be me.

He recalled the goal perfectly! He said, 'It was a great run and cross by David White, but as the ball came in, I've realised I can't hit it with my right, so I decided to have a go with my knee, and it was a fantastic finish.'

The journo wrote down every word and a few days later, a friend of my uncle sent a news clipping from *The Times* quoting Brian verbatim. Well, if you're a reporter and you can't tell the difference between me and Brian Gayle, maybe you should be in a different job!

So I had a look around Dean Court and I must admit, it had quite a welcoming feel to it all. I met manager Harry

Redknapp, and chatted with Brian Tiler, who did most of the talking. During our conversation, Luther Blissett popped in to say hello. He said, 'Get your arse down here!' He said he'd been impressed each time he'd played in games against me, and he'd love to play up front with me. The fact that he'd come out of his way to see me made a big impression as he was a striker I had always looked up to and I remember thinking, 'Imagine playing up front with him.'

Here was a legend of the English game, a former Watford icon, AC Milan striker and England forward and I just imagined how much I could learn from him. In all my 21 years, I'd never had a striker coach or someone who could help me develop my game, but here was an opportunity to take advice from one of the best and, at 31, he still had plenty of mileage left in him. It was because of Luther that I decided to sign for Bournemouth.

They offered me two possible options for a place to live – one was an apartment on the seafront and the other was living in digs with a family and a couple of other young Bournemouth players. I decided to move into digs and settled in pretty quickly.

I was happy because Bournemouth had ambition and were signing players who could give promotion a real go. Luther had been there a year, plus there was Paul Miller, Gerry Peyton, Gavin Peacock, Phil Kite, and they also had Shaun

Brooks – one of the best passers of a ball I'd ever seen. They were giving promotion a real go and had put their money where their mouth was and given Harry the funds to bring in some top-class pros.

I was finally getting paid what I thought I was worth, too! Ian Bishop, by coincidence, left Bournemouth and moved to City, but it wasn't a swap deal as I was almost a free agent without a club, and I think Bish signed later in the summer for about £465,000. Would I have enjoyed playing alongside him? Definitely.

I had some catching up to do as my ankle still wasn't right. I was OK to run on it, but if I didn't catch the ball right, it was a bit sore, which I just put down to wear and tear – no such thing as MRI scans in those days.

I was a bit rusty and a bit stiff, but nothing I couldn't live with, though a lot of the early enthusiasm I had about the move was dampened by a terrible pre-season when I don't think we won a single game. Everyone was twitching about it. We went to Wales on a tour and won nothing, and the lads weren't gelling for some reason.

Then I picked up a blister that turned into an ulcer which kept me out for a week or so before we finally had our first league game of the season, away to Brighton. I think I hit the woodwork twice and Luther did as well – we could have beaten them by five or six, but we actually lost 2-1.

Despite the defeat, there had been enough that day to suggest things were starting to come together and in our next game at home to West Brom, I scored my first Bournemouth goal in a 1-1 draw. Four days later we beat Hull 5-4, then drew away to Ipswich Town before beating promotion favourites Newcastle United 2-1 at Dean Court. We'd shown what we were capable of, and I was happy and enjoying life – plus I wasn't looking over my shoulder all the time worrying about being dropped.

But there was one issue I had to deal with – and that was Shaun Teale.

Teale had broken my ankle in my penultimate game for City the previous season. It was a bad challenge, he went right over the ball but that happened in football and as far as I was concerned, that was the end of it. He was going to be my team-mate now, so I expected we'd have a bit of banter about it. Maybe he'd even apologise and that would be that – but for whatever reason, it was far from over for Teale.

I'd very quickly become close to Paul Miller, Gerry Peyton, Shaun Brooks and Luther and after each session, we'd go and have lunch; it was a completely different culture from City. Collectively we discussed the apparent friction between Teale and myself it was obvious to all that Teale was out for me for whatever reason. They saw things with Teale that I didn't. We'd had a few sessions of forwards versus defenders and, though I hadn't really thought about it, Teale had been shadowing me in those sessions and whenever he could putting 'enthusiastic' challenges in. It didn't bother me as I'd had that all my life and I didn't mind the competitive edge as it was more realistic to what you'd get in a game, so long as there was no malice – but that's exactly what my new team-mates thought there was. They told me to watch my back and be careful.

Teale was your typical centre-half of the day; he wanted to kick everybody in sight but wasn't too happy when he got kicked back! I didn't like him as a person but would have just got on with it and been professional as we were team-mates now, but for whatever reason it was, he had taken a major dislike to me and that would rumble throughout my time with the club.

I kept an eye on City's results and saw they'd beaten United 5-1 at Maine Road, which pleased me no end as a fan, but I didn't want Machin to succeed at my club and when, just six weeks later, City were dicked 6-0 by Derby County, he was sacked. Hallelujah. I think chairman Peter Swales said it was because he had a lack of rapport with the City fans and I was thinking, 'Fuck me, the bloke had the personality of a door and had no rapport with the players, either.'

His dismissal also made me feel sad – not for him as I honestly couldn't have given two fucks about Mel Machin (as you've no doubt gathered by this point) – because the nagging voice at the back of my mind kept asking, 'What if?' What if I'd signed a month-to-month contract (if I'd have said I couldn't find another club, this had been one of my options back in June) and just ground it out with City? If I had, by that stage I'd have had a new manager coming in and a blank page to work with.

I was even more gutted when Howard Kendall was named the new City boss. Would Kendall have remembered the tackle he made when I went on trial to Everton that left me with a gashed shin? Would he have remembered me playing on and telling me, 'That's what we like here – tough lads'? I'll never know, but I think he'd have given me a chance because he didn't fancy most of the forwards Machin had assembled at the club. He brought in Adrian Heath and Wayne Clarke, and could I have done as well as either of those two? I'd like to think so, but that ship had well and truly sailed and while things might well have been different had I gritted my teeth and seen it through, I didn't sit up all night letting it eat away at me.

I was playing regularly again, scoring goals and was happy where I was.

I'd also developed a great understanding with Shaun Brooks, who was a ridiculously talented midfielder. I'd say a lot of my goals came from passes from Shaun or moves started by him. In one game, to illustrate that understanding, we were home to Oldham and were awarded a free kick about 30 yards out. I glanced at Shaun over my shoulder, and he immediately took a quick free kick, spotting my run and curling a ball into the space in front of me about four feet high where I launched on to it and headed it past the keeper in a 2-0 win. Sometimes you just find players like that who get you, and you get them. I had the same with Julian Darby at Bolton Lads – it wasn't telepathy or any of that, it was just a connection that's hard to explain.

I ripped Oldham apart that day, something that would stick in their manager Joe Royle's mind as events later in the season would suggest, but it wasn't the goal that had pleased me no end – it had been the fact I'd been up against one of my best mates in football, Earl Barrett, and I'd given him the sweetest nutmeg I'd ever done. Gerry Peyton pinged the ball into me, I brought it down and my next touch took the ball through Earl's legs, and I could almost hear him die inside as I did it. A few of the lads said after the game, 'Fucking hell, you enjoyed that didn't you?' and I just told them it had been one of my best moments in football! Even now, whenever I see Earl, I laugh because I know he knows what's coming as I remind him about that day, but what a great defender he was.

The season was going OK, but we just couldn't buy a win away from home. Our results at Dean Court were good and if we'd matched them with results on the road, we'd have been there or thereabouts, but by the turn of the year we'd won just one of our ten away games, taking only six points from a possible 30. It was around then that I hit a sticky period of my own, but that was purely down to the fact that Redknapp wasn't playing Shaun Brooks. He'd been dropped and had a bit of an injury and the style of play changed as a result, with balls knocked long and over the top instead of playing to feet or into the channels. Shaun didn't tackle and as we were starting to struggle Redknapp went with a more combative style which just didn't suit the players we had – in my opinion.

There were a few reasons we fell away that season and the lack of facilities at the club, I felt, were fundamental to everything. We'd train on the large grassy area in front of Dean Court or in the park. When we had shooting practice, there were no nets so there was this guy who used to ride his bike to go and fetch the balls for us. It was mad. He was Hungarian and we learned he'd been a former professional footballer in his homeland and actually was quite a knowledgeable bloke. One day, we were having some lunch in the café in the park, and he wandered in, so a few of the lads started having the craic with him and he asked us, 'Why do you always shoot when your legs are fresh?' He said we should run and run and run and then have shooting practice when our legs were tired which would better replicate game-type situations. Just simple advice that made perfect sense when you actually sat down and thought about it. Some of the things he said blew us away – he should have been on the coaching staff if you ask me.

I had a cortisone injection in my ankle in early January and was fit for the game away to Hull where I was up against Richard Shaw, who had been loaned from Crystal Palace. What a player he was! While he was kicking two lumps of shit out of me throughout the game, I was giving as good as I got and was loving it. It was a proper ding-dong battle, but at half-time, our coach Jimmy Gable told me to calm down because I would get sent off. It was six of one, half a dozen of the other, but eventually I was hauled off and Jamie Redknapp made his debut to replace me. It was the first time in my career I'd been taken off for playing aggressively! To me, it was just a good, hard duel. We won 4-1 and I was a bit miffed, but I let it go.

The season slowly began to deteriorate thereafter – partly because I felt there were lads who weren't being picked but were better than the ones who actually were playing – that's just how I saw it. But my time on the south coast was about to end abruptly.

The friction with Shaun Teale had never really gone away and I had the distinct impression that if he had the chance to do me, he'd have taken it. I don't know that for a fact, but that was the feeling I had. The bad feeling festered on until we had this one training session when, as I recall, Harry Redknapp wasn't there for some reason. Jimmy Gable took it, and it was the same old stuff – a bit of passing and then a five-a-side game. The surface was poor and as the game went on, the ball bounced between me and Teale, and it was one of those moments when your career flashes in front of your eyes. I knew in an instant that it was either him or me. He was going to do me, I could see it in his eyes that he'd been waiting for that moment, so before he could, I went high and caught him under his knee. It was a bad tackle that did his cruciate ligament. It's fair to say it was either him or me. And this time it wasn't going to be me.

Redknapp went mad when he found out Teale was out for the rest of the season, which was understandable. He also had doubts about my ankle. It had never been right since Teale's tackle at Maine Road. My tackle on Shaun sort of spelled the end for me at Bournemouth. Harry needed money for new players ahead of the transfer deadline in late March and he made it clear that it was either Gavin Peacock to Newcastle United or me to Oldham Athletic and was a case of whoever put money down first.

We actually played Oldham on Tuesday, 20 March 1990, and they were going well in the League Cup having just knocked West Ham United out, so they were now in the final against Nottingham Forest. They had also got an FA Cup semi-final coming up against Manchester United, so while they might have been in the Second Division they were one of the best teams outside the top flight. Frankie Bunn had been their main striker, but his back was knackered because of the AstroTurf at Boundary Park, and they needed cover. We travelled up the day before and, on the coach, Harry pulled me to one side and told me I'd be signing for Oldham and that I'd played my last game for Bournemouth. That was that.

I wasn't that bothered if truth be told because Oldham were a better prospect on paper, and I'd be back near my family again. I let my dad know and he said he'd come over for the contract negotiations.

We were staying at Mottram Hall in Cheshire and Harry told me I needed to go and speak to Joe Royle. It was a good 25 miles away and I had no way of getting there under my own steam. Luther Blissett told me I should get a cab and charge it to the club, so I did. I went to Boundary Park, the deal was agreed, and I sat out the game the next night with Oldham winning 4-0.

The transfer fee was about £260,000, which I believe was a record at the time for Latics – and my currency was good because everyone wants a goalscorer don't they?

As a footnote to my time at Bournemouth, as recently as 2021, Teale is still bleating on about that tackle I made on him. I'd just like to say this, 'Shaun, yeah, it was a really bad challenge, but no worse than the one you made on me at Maine Road the year before. In football terms, one each! Move on, mate.'

My one season with Bournemouth saw me play 37 games and score 13 goals. I signed for Oldham on transfer deadline day and Bournemouth lost the majority of their last 16 games, winning just once, and got relegated with the infamous home game against Leeds United on the final day where thousands of ticketless Leeds fans rioted on a hot bank holiday weekend on the south coast. Could I have helped save them? Maybe – but we'll never know.

I enjoyed my time with the club, and I was sorry to see them go down, but now I had to focus on my move back to the north-west and a new chapter with Joe Royle's Oldham.

16

The Yard Dog

THERE WAS one thing about my move to Oldham I wasn't looking forward to. I would have to get used to playing on a plastic pitch, which was never going to be good for my ankles or knees as there was no give in it. It was sharp, lively and fast and it took a lot of adjusting to. It wasn't like the 3G pitches of today – it was like rolling a carpet over a car park and then playing football on it. And the more I played on it, the worse my ankle got.

I played the remainder of the 1989/90 season, getting a game here and there as we finished eighth in the Second Division, but the team had done ever so well in the cup competitions and that probably cost them promotion.

I could have been part of Oldham Athletic being kicked out of the FA Cup had I kept my mouth shut. They were playing Manchester United at Maine Road in the semi-final, and I'd been named on the bench for the game on the Sunday.

The problem was, I'd already played in the FA Cup with Bournemouth that season (18 minutes as sub appearance at Wolves), so as I was walking back off the training pitch with Paul Warhurst and Earl Barrett, I said, 'I've already played in the cup this year. But a semi-final at Maine Road? Come on. If the FA find out, they're not going to kick Oldham out at the semi-final stage, are they?'

Paul and Earl shot around and told me I had to tell the gaffer that I was cup-tied but even then, I was thinking I might try and wing it and I might not get caught, but those two told me I'd get the club kicked out and talked a bit of sense into me. I went to see Joe and told him I'd already played in the FA Cup and he went to see the secretary to give him a bollocking. Joe said to me, 'That's why we bought you – to play in the cup competitions.'

What a game to miss. The first match ended 3-3 and then United won the replay 2-1, but I was sat in the stands watching both of them.

My first full season with the Latics, 1990/91, saw us blow everyone away on the way to winning the title and promotion, but my ankle was getting worse and worse and nobody could work out what the problem was.

I did OK that year but was in and out of the team with the odd goal here and there – nothing spectacular. Andy Ritchie and Ian Marshall were firing on all cylinders at the time, scoring plenty of goals, so opportunities were few and far between.

I had to take the chances that came, but in one game, Joe played me as an outside-right when Neil Adams was injured, and I had a shocker as we lost 2-1 away to Hull City. I'm many things, but I'm not a right-winger!

We beat Sheffield Wednesday on the last day of the season to go up as champions, but by the following pre-season my ankle was becoming a major issue and it got so bad that I couldn't play.

I'd miss most of our First Division season – this was the final year before the Premier League started – as a result, and for seven months I was putting my foot in a bucket of ice water each morning, but nothing was getting done. I'd been to several hospitals around the country but yet again, I had an injury nobody could cure or figure out exactly what it was.

I'd missed virtually the whole of the 1991/92 season, and I lost my head at the time. I was sure Oldham wanted an insurance for me which meant retirement for me and a payout for them. It got to the stage where Joe Royle came and saw the physio and had an argument over me. He was frustrated and probably thought he'd bought a crock. He said, 'Right, you're going to Lilleshall for two weeks.' He thought he was punishing me, but I just said, 'Hallelujah!' By this time, I'd had 13 cortisone injections in my right ankle over a six-month period, but I was confident they'd put me right at Lilleshall. They had specialists in long-term injuries, and I knew they would investigate the issue thoroughly, but after a fortnight of X-rays, soft tissue scans and examinations from various experts, they also had to admit they couldn't find the cause of the pain and the swelling. That was the worst possible outcome for me because now it looked like there wasn't any actual injury and it appeared to everyone that I was either swinging a leg or it was all in my head.

I went back to Oldham and Joe was majorly pissed off. He said, 'Right – last chance. You're going to see a surgeon called Tony Banks in Bolton.' I said to Joe that if this guy was any good, being from Bolton and having had the injuries I'd had over the past ten years, I'd have known about him. But I was at my wits' end and would have seen a witch doctor if I'd thought they could sort me out. I was a lost cause on the verge of being forced to retire at the age of 23, so I had nothing to lose.

It turned out that Tony Banks was my saviour and, for me, my manna from heaven. He didn't just identify the problem and then operate, he took a genuine interest in me as a person and my ongoing recovery afterwards. Within a month, he had me playing again.

At my first meeting with Tony, he told me to take my tracksuit bottoms off plus my socks and trainers. He then lay on the floor in his best suit, shirt and tie as I walked up and down as instructed. He told me there was nothing wrong with the way I was walking and asked me to go across the road and get an X-ray done. I brought the X-rays back with me and he looked at them and said, 'It's that beak there – it just needs taking off.' He pointed to one of the images where he could see a spike of bone had developed on the front of my shin. He told me that this was the cause of all the problems – and that's all it was. I'd seen five or six specialists over the past seven months but none of them had solved it, yet Tony had sussed it out in an hour. He told me that it was due to the fracture I received at Maine Road against Bournemouth not being put in plaster which had caused it not to heal correctly.

I had the operation, and my mum and dad came to see me afterwards and Tony came in still in his scrubs not long after they arrived. He said hello to them both and my dad said, 'Hello, Mr Banks.' He replied, 'It's Tony.' Then he looked over at me. 'I've heard this lad is half decent – just weak as piss.'

I was thinking, 'Cheeky get!' and he then said that I needed to get beefed up a bit. Tony was an Olympic weightlifter and shortly after he invited me along to the gym where he trained at the Forum in Wythenshawe. It was here that I met a lot of his mates, who were streetwise, you could say, but good lads and as strong as oxes.

A funny thing happened at one of those sessions and it had nothing to do with me getting stronger. A lad called Kev came in; he was going mad saying that the plastering gang he worked in had been shafted by two lads who had left him high and dry to go and 'play in a band' – I've never seen anyone as angry, but it was understandable; it was his livelihood he was talking about.

Guess what! Two years later Kev invited me to go watch Oasis, the band his two lads had left for, at Maine Road! Kev was still plastering in New Zealand the last time I spoke to him – I'm not sure what the Gallagher brothers are up to though, right now!

My ankle felt good again, but Banksy had me doing weights as soon as I could and then asked if I was free to join him at Leverhulme Park in Bolton one Sunday. He said he had a few lads he'd operated on and wanted to see how we were all progressing. I arrived and Steve McMahon, Niall Quinn and Andy Walker among others were all there with a bag of balls. He wanted to check everything was spot on. That was what set him apart from other surgeons – that genuine interest in you as a person and the ongoing input to ensure your recovery was the best it could be.

A dad with his lad walked past and the kid said, 'Dad, there's Niall Quinn and Steve McMahon.' I heard him say something along the lines of, 'Why would Niall Quinn be in Leverhulme Park at half nine on a Sunday morning?' It was so funny!

Tony saved my career when Oldham had been more than ready to write me off. I wasn't match fit, but I was running and training again and it was hilarious because Joe was following me around the training pitch for the last two weeks of the season saying, 'You're going to Norway, you're going to Norway.' It turned out he wanted me to play for Molde during the summer to get my sharpness back. I didn't need to go to bleeding Norway, I just needed a good pre-season and to continue my running sessions with Robbie Brightwell, but he wouldn't take no for an answer, while I was like, 'What the fuck do I want to go there for?'

Then, I think it was for the last game of the season, we were at home to City, and I didn't even look at the team sheet when it was put up but one of the lads said, 'Fucking hell, Mouldy – you're on the bench!' And I was. I came on and late on I tapped home a late consolation in a 5-2 defeat. I wasn't really match fit, but I'd played and scored, which felt good, even if it was against City.

The following Monday, I went to see Joe and we argued again about me going to Molde, but it was an argument I was never going to win.

A few days later, I was on a plane to Norway. Molde were a month or so into their season and when I landed, I was picked up at the airport and taken to the club to sign some papers. I went to see the chairman who glanced up at me and said something in Norwegian. The guy who collected me was there throughout so I asked what the chairman had said and he said he'd tell me after – which he did – and it turns out he said, 'I didn't know he was that small.' The cheek!

Arthur Albiston, formerly of Manchester United, was also at Molde and I would be staying with him during my time in Norway. He was a great fella and while I was chatting with him on that first day, another lad walked in who was about 6ft 7in tall and was also a ski jumper (and what a loose cannon he turned out to be!). It turned out that was who I'd been brought in to replace as he was injured. They thought because I had scored in the First Division, they were getting Mark Hughes or something, and in the local papers they'd found out about my schoolboy world records so I think they expected me to score five goals every game. Nobody had mentioned my schoolboy stats for about eight years, but the local Norwegian papers had dug it out from God knows where and now I had that albatross around my neck, which pissed me off no end.

Scoring goals for Bolton Lads was a thing of the past and while it was nice to see my name in the *Guinness Book of Records*, it also brought with it one or two caveats, meaning that people who hadn't followed my career thought I was some sort of goalscoring phenomenon. It had pretty much been forgotten back home, but now I was in Norway where people were seeing it with fresh eyes and wondering why I wasn't scoring a bagful every game, but the reason I wasn't was because I wasn't fully fit.

Norwegian football was played at pace, it was physical, and the players were strong. It was a good standard, but I didn't want to be there. I wanted to get back home because I knew what to do, who to work with and how to manage my own body. I'd been doing it for years.

Arthur sat down with me and said, 'How do you feel about being here?' I said I didn't want to be in Norway, and it became clear that there was a discrepancy on the money I was being paid. I'll not go into details, but let's just say I wasn't given the wage I should have been because of reasons I can't go into.

Norway was so expensive. We were getting taxed at about 54 per cent and I actually couldn't afford to pay the mortgage on my house back in Bolton and the bills that needed paying as well. So not only was my heart not in it but I felt like I was paying for the privilege of being there.

The language barrier didn't help either, plus they had one or two rules in games that were different – but nobody told me! I found out the hard way in my first match when the opposition keeper passed a goal kick out to a defender on his left and I ran across the edge of the penalty area to go and close him down. The lad I was approaching stopped dead and I took the ball and crossed it into the middle. The referee blew his whistle, said something I didn't understand and awarded a free kick against me. I had no idea why, so the next time it happened I did the same thing again and, before I got anywhere near, the ref blew again but, this time, he raced up to me brandishing a yellow card!

I went in at the break and said, 'What the fuck?' I was running my bollocks off and wanted to get fit and do my best, even if I did want to be elsewhere. The manager was having a go at me, and I asked Arthur if he knew what he was on about. He didn't, so they brought in a guy who could interpret and the gist of it was, the manager was saying they had different rules from England! My response to that was, 'Well, don't you think someone should have fucking told me before I played?' After we'd sorted the language barrier, the best was yet to come. I'd spied a tub of cut oranges, at least that's what I thought they were – I did think they looked a bit pale – turns out they were lemons, as I found out as I sucked one. Arthur just shook his head!

Arthur and I lived a humble lifestyle and would have an ice cream by the sea on a Friday night because we couldn't afford anything else, and I wondered what the lads back home would make of it all. I got a bit fitter with Molde before returning to Oldham where Joe had seen his arse over something or other. He said, 'You won't be playing in the first team this season, you won't get a game with the reserves, and I'm loathe to play you in the A team because we've got good kids coming through, so you're going on loan.'

I thought, 'Here we go' – people would be assuming that it was me, that I'd spat my dummy out and didn't want to do this or that, but anyone who really knows me knows I just wanted to play football and score goals.

I was clearly finished at Oldham, so I just said to Joe, 'OK, where am I going then?' He said it was either Plymouth or Brighton and I just looked at him, thinking, 'For fuck's sake – you couldn't get me any further away!' I said, 'What colour do Plymouth play in?' He said green, so then I asked what colour Brighton played in. I did know, but he said 'blue and white stripes' so I said, 'Right, I've never played in blue and white stripes, so I'll go there.' And that's how I made the decision. The atmosphere in Joe's office had been toxic so it was just a bit of a piss-take from my side, but regardless of that, I was now on my way back to the south coast.

What was Joe's problem? Did he think I'd gone there with an injury that I should have told them about? Possibly. But I'd gone to Bournemouth with the same injury so I thought any issues would be picked up in the medical. Was that his beef? I honestly don't know. The medical treatment I received at Oldham was poor and I think they thought being injured was a sign of weakness. I believe some of the medical staff's opinions fuelled Joe's anger towards me. Maybe they thought

I was soft because I had this continuous swelling around my ankle, but I was in constant pain, and I could barely turn. I remembered I'd been playing a practice game about a year before and Richard Jobson said, 'What's up, Paul? You're a bit shy.' I told him my ankle was fucked, and he went and told Joe, saying, 'Gaffer, he's proper struggling here.' But I'm not sure Joe ever really believed it.

It was time to pack my bags again and head south.

17

Brighton Rock

WHAT A breath of fresh sea air my loan spell with Brighton and Hove Albion turned out to be. It was exactly what I needed at the time and would turn out to be one of the most enjoyable periods of my career, despite it being only a three-month deal.

Joe Royle told me to get on with it, so on the Thursday before the start of the 1993/94 season, I travelled down in my car for a meeting at 5pm with club officials. I ended up arriving at 2am the next day following a big crash on the M25. I didn't know where I was going, so I called my dad and he found the address of the hotel I would be staying at and, thankfully, they'd stayed up for me, so I checked in and got my head down.

I woke up early wondering where I was at first, and then went downstairs for breakfast where two other new signings, Steve Cotterill and Andy Kennedy, were already eating. I didn't know them from Adam, but I was introduced to them both, had something to eat and then set off to sign the loan papers and then it was on to training.

The last 48 hours had been a whirlwind and I hadn't had time to even think about anything, but I quickly found there was a great group of lads at the club who made me feel welcome from the moment I arrived. The manager was Barry Lloyd, and his assistant was Martin Hinshelwood, and they wanted to put me straight into the team for the game away to Leyton Orient the next day.

I was determined to get back right on it again and make the most of my time there, but I was still a bit short of match fitness and sharpness. Before we kicked off I discovered we were warming up with Adidas Tango balls, which I loved because they had a sweet spot that I knew how to find. They were brilliant. The usual Mitre ball didn't have the same appeal because although it had its own sweet spot, it was much harder to find. At kick-off, sure enough we were using the Adidas Tango which pleased me no end. The first half at Orient was OK, but I wasn't happy with my contribution and was determined to somehow make my mark on my debut.

So, in the second half, I picked the ball up about 35 yards out, found that sweet spot and hit a shot that went one way and then the other and the keeper, Chris Turner, didn't have a chance as it flew past him into the net. A goal in my first game was as good as I could have hoped for, but we lost 3-2 so it was a case of swings and roundabouts on this occasion.

It was a decent start and after such a bad time at Oldham, it was exactly what I needed. The goal had settled my nerves and I'd done well after the enforced break from playing so I just felt like a weight had been lifted off my shoulders and I actually felt part of something again for the first time in a couple of seasons.

I wasn't allowed to play in cup matches as part of my agreement, so I missed the midweek League Cup tie against Colchester United, something that didn't sit well with me after the conversation I had with Joe Royle about not being good enough to play in any team at Oldham, so what was the problem? My next game would be my home debut against – of all clubs – Bolton Wanderers.

I found out where Bolton were staying and told Steve Cotterill that I was going to have a walk up the seafront to have a chat with a few of my old buddies. It would also be the first time I'd played against my old Bolton Lads team-mate Julian Darby so it would be good to have a quick catch-up ahead of the game the next day.

Steve came with me after tea and as I approached their hotel, Julian, Tony Kelly and a couple of other Bolton players were just coming out for a stroll in their club tracksuits.

Julian saw me and said, 'All right, Mouldy! What are you doing down here?' I told him I was at Brighton for a few months and had come over for a quick natter, so we all had a walk down the promenade with the sea lapping at the shore in the distance. Steve didn't know anyone from the Bolton team, but he was your archetypal chirpy chap. Tony, a more than decent playmaker who could open your team up with one pass and likeable Scouser to boot, started chattering away like he always did, when Steve said, 'Hey, Driver – shut it. Nobody's talking to you.' It turned out Steve thought Tony was the team's coach driver!

Tony was like, 'Eh, what the fuck?'

I said, 'He didn't say anything Tony, we're just on our way,' cutting it short before he realised what he meant.

Tony wasn't your most athletic-looking footballer, but he was a great player and I said to Steve, 'He'll make you pay for that tomorrow – he can pass like a fucking demon.'

Steve said, 'Who the fuck is he? He's a big 'un to be playing football. He should be driving the fucking team coach.' This was just one of many memorable moments with Steve and Andy Kennedy on the south coast.

As it was, we beat Bolton 2-1 and though I didn't do anything spectacular, it was good to get off to a winning start in my first game at the Goldstone Ground. It was the first time I'd ever faced my hometown club but, as I say, I didn't really do anything special, which is a pity.

I was cup-tied for the return leg against Colchester, then we travelled to Bradford, and then Exeter City – I scored in that game – before we were back at the Goldstone to play Preston North End.

As I parked up in the players' and officials' car park, the chairman had just arrived in his brand-new green Lotus. He must have seen me staring at it because he called over, 'You like that, Paul?' I said I did, laughing, and he said, 'Are you going back home after the game?' I said I was heading back to Bolton for a few days, and he said, 'Right, get a hat-trick and you can go home in the Lotus, and I'll have yours for a couple of days.'

I was thinking that I had rarely, if ever, spoken to the chairman of a club I was at and here's this guy offering me his Lotus if I bagged a treble. It was refreshing if I'm honest.

I scored twice early on against Preston and was working my bollocks off to get a third, shooting from everywhere and anywhere – I don't think anyone else had a shot! But that third wouldn't go in for me, we won 2-0 and I drove home in my own car that night. Still, as incentives go, it had done the trick!

I was playing well, scoring again, and felt good and confident for the first time in a long time. I bagged another in a 2-2 draw away to Blackpool and everyone was saying what a great header it was, even though it had come off my shoulder. I just went along with it, but when the goals were shown on TV on Monday night, the lads were all calling me a fraud and I just said, 'Well, you've got to be in it to win it.'

We'd played Bradford, Preston, Bolton and Blackpool in the first few weeks, and Steve Foster, the big centre-half who always wore a headband to keep his long curly hair out of his eyes – and someone who I'd never met prior to my move – was always trying to have a bit of fun, saying, 'Northerners, you're all wankers,' in the worst Mancunian accent you've ever heard.

After the Blackpool game we got on the coach, when Foster spotted an old guy waiting outside the ground with a raincoat, flat cap and a greyhound on a lead. He said, 'Eh, Mouldy – your grandad's here!' What he didn't know was that my grandad really had come to watch that afternoon.

I laughed and said, 'Fuck off, Steve.'

He went on, 'They've all got greyhounds or whippets up here, lad.'

About five feet to this guy's left, actually was my grandad, in a raincoat with a flat cap on! He was next to my mum and dad, so I said, 'That's my grandad, Fozzy.'

He looked to where I was pointing and said, 'Fuck off, that's not your grandad!' As the coach pulled away, I banged on the window and my grandad put his thumb up and waved back and Steve went, 'It IS your fucking grandad! Where's his greyhound?'

That went on all week, so I decided to have a bit of fun of my own. Rod, the Brighton chef, was also the chef at my hotel and a good lad, so I said, 'Rod, do you know anyone who owns a greyhound?'

He said, 'Yeah, actually I do – my best mate has one, why?'

I asked whether I'd be able to borrow it on Saturday. He asked if I was playing so I said I was, and the dog would need to be at the ground for half past one. He said I was barmy, but he'd sort it out.

On matchday, I met his mate outside and gave him a couple of tickets, before leading the dog to the home dressing room where I put a flat cap on him. He was sat in Steve Foster's place and one of the lads said I should stick Fozzy's number five shirt on the dog, which I did, and he just sat there in his shirt with a flat cap on, good as gold! Fozzy loved it and had to admit I'd done him there.

Then the gaffer came in early and saw the dog's arse and told me to get him, but everyone was pissing themselves laughing. We had to play in pink shirts that day as I think Reading arrived without a change of strip and as they were in blue and white hoops, they clashed with our home shirts. It was baking hot, but it turned out that Fozzy had an allergic reaction to the dog hair and broke out in a rash all over his back. He was red raw and had to jump in a cold bath at half-time to calm his skin down. The gaffer was furious. We ended up losing 1-0, so maybe it wasn't the best idea, although I think the difference on the day wasn't the dog but the fact Shaka Hislop was outstanding in goal all afternoon.

A few days before that, we were due to play Manchester United in the League Cup and the gaffer had come in and said to me I couldn't play because Oldham weren't allowing it. I'd been there for about six weeks, had been scoring and playing well and Joe Royle, who'd made it clear my time at Oldham was over, was stopping me playing against United in case I was needed back at Boundary Park.

As a result, I did an article in the *Manchester Evening News* saying that I didn't think Royle should have it both ways and that he'd all but said I wasn't playing for Oldham again, yet I now wasn't allowed to play against United. How did that work? I said it was one or the other and that I felt he couldn't have it both ways. The interview went down like the proverbial lead balloon at Oldham.

Could I understand the thinking? I suppose if I had scored against United at the Goldstone Ground – which had a slope I loved – while Oldham were struggling in the Premier League, people would have been asking questions. To people outside, they would have probably thought something along the lines of Oldham paid my wages so they could do what they liked, but they hadn't been privy to the conversation I'd had with Joe when he'd spelled out the situation to me in no uncertain terms.

Any part of the bridge at Oldham that was still left was probably burned that day but I was enjoying life at Brighton and would have happily signed a permanent deal right there and then. Instead, what would be my last game for the Seagulls was against Wigan Athletic – a 1-0 win – and my loan spell was suddenly over.

I'd scored five goals in 11 games – not bad considering I couldn't get a game at any level for my parent club – and my stay there had restored my faith in my own ability to play and make an impact again. I can't speak highly enough about Brighton & Hove Albion as a club, and the players, officials and supporters were all fantastic towards me.

I remember before the final game, I spoke with *Grandstand* presenter Des Lynam who I think held some honorary board role at Brighton. I was taken up to the directors' box where I was thanked for everything I'd done for the club. He asked me how much I was on at Oldham, and I told him. He said they couldn't afford that but could probably put a package together for me and I said, 'Right, great.'

But I never heard a dicky bird and neither did Steve Cotterill, who had also been on loan and had done well. It was bizarre, and I have no clue to this day what happened.

The reality was that I had to go back to the place I least wanted to be and back to a manager who wanted me out. Nothing had changed when I got back and despite me proving my fitness and that I could score goals, everything was just as it was, and mentally, it was like torture. The weeks passed like Groundhog Day and all the enthusiasm and confidence I'd built back up at Brighton slowly drained away.

I went in every Friday to ask for a transfer that was turned down each and every time and I still wasn't playing but I did have one reserve game for Latics and afterwards, I went in to see Joe Royle and Jim Cassell, the chief scout. Jim said, 'Come in, Paul, come in – the gaffer will be here in a few minutes.'

I sat down and he said, 'I watched you in the reserves on Tuesday and thought you did really well. You're back on it again.' And I was. I was trying my bollocks off to get a move if nothing else, but in walked Royle and he said, 'I thought you were poor Tuesday night, what did you think, Jim?'

Jim said, 'Yeah, I thought you were poor.'

It was like mental torture, and I was reaching the end of my tether. Then, one day, I finally lost it completely. I loved Willie Donachie, Joe's number two. I had nothing but respect for him because he was an absolute top fella and he ensured I stayed fit when I was training away from the first team.

This particular day, I was walking past Willie and he said, 'Mouldy, we're one short for five-a-side, come and join in.' So, I did. We started playing and because there were no keepers, I ran back and blocked a shot on the line. The other team shouted, 'Penalty, penalty!' I hadn't used anything other than my lower body but Willie shouted, 'Yeah, Mouldy, you cheated! Penalty!'

Then the red mist descended. Willie could have said that at almost any other time in my life and I would have laughed it off, but not at that moment. Everything I'd been through in the past two and a half years suddenly boiled up inside me and I exploded at him.

I think he realised I'd lost it when I gave him a few choice words and I just walked off. He came to the changing rooms to try and pacify me, saying it was just a comment and it was – but unbeknown to him, it was just the wrong time. I said, 'I've had it up to here, Willie. I'm done. I just want to play football in a first team somewhere, score some goals and be happy.'

Willie said, because I'd walked off, he'd have to go and tell the gaffer and I said, 'Fine, tell him then, let's get it sorted out once and for all.'

Joe came down and I stood my ground. He could see I'd flipped and said, 'We'll get you out as quick as we can.'

Speaking to Willie Donachie the way I did is one of the biggest regrets in my life because he was such a great coach and a great fella too.

I took a few days, but on the last day of the March 1993 transfer deadline, Joe told me Birmingham City had come in for me, offering the asking price on a permanent deal.

I was so desperate to get away that I would have walked the 80-odd miles to sign for them.

18

Once Upon a Time in the Midlands

I HAD no idea where Birmingham City were in the league. They were in what is now the Championship, but I hadn't a clue how they were doing.

I have a friend called Robert Campbell and he helped and advised me with my affairs when needed. Robert came with me to Birmingham, and we arrived before midday with the March transfer window closing later that evening.

We went tp St Andrew's where I met the Birmingham manager Terry Cooper, who had played for Leeds United in the early 1970s as a left-back – what a smashing bloke and I was absolutely blown away by him. It was like talking to my dad or my grandad because he was so down to earth, honest and considerate. We had a good chat, and everything seemed great and then Trevor Morgan, Cooper's number two, popped in to say hello. As an ex-Bolton Wanderers player, we had a sort of common bond and we hit it off straight away.

Cooper said, if I joined, I'd be one of seven lads they were bringing in on deadline day, one of whom was Andy Saville. I knew Andy from his days at Walsall and I had always rated him as a striker. I was impressed by everything Cooper had to say, his vision for the club, the role he wanted me to play in it and at the end, I said, 'Thanks, Terry, I'll go away and have a think.'

But time was of the essence and Cooper said I'd need to let them know fairly quickly with the deadline looming so I promised I'd get back to him as soon as I'd had time to have a chat with Robert, and maybe my dad, and just get my head around it all.

Robert and I got back in the car and on to the M6 and I asked what he'd thought. He said, 'Paul, they're 12 points adrift at the bottom of the league. In a couple of months, that means you'll be playing in the Third Division.'

I said, 'Didn't you get the same good vibes I did?'

He said, 'The only thing I got out of it all was that you're a Premier League player now, so you'll effectively be dropping down two divisions.'

I didn't say much to Robert after that as I had too much spinning around my head. Finally we got to Knutsford Services for a coffee and I told him I wanted to call Terry Cooper and go over one or two things that were jumping out at me.

Robert said if I was doing that – and if I was intent on signing for Birmingham – I should ask for a few more quid and get a better deal for myself as I would probably be a third-tier player in a few months.

But I wasn't thinking of money. I was thinking of the chat I'd had with Cooper and the impression he'd made on me. My gut instinct was that this was the right move for me, but I just needed to be sure.

I phoned Terry and told him the one or two issues I had, and he just said, 'Paul, look, you've got to buy into me and what we are trying to do here. You don't know that much about me but ask your dad. He'll tell you that when I played, I always tried and gave my all and that's what I'm going to do here to try to get Birmingham out of this mess. If you want to come and play for me, come and play, but if you don't, I understand, but it's been really nice meeting you.'

It was that last line that convinced me I wanted to play for him.

I told him I was going to turn back around and sign for Birmingham and he said he was really pleased to hear that, but added I needed to sign the contract before midnight. I joined Robert who was having a coffee while he waited and he nearly spat his drink out when I told him I'd told them I was going to sign. He asked what had made me so certain and I told him he'd said that if I didn't sign that it had been nice meeting me.

He raised his eyebrows and said, 'At the end of the day, it's up to you, Paul. You know my thoughts.'

I told him that football wasn't just black and white and that there was no way I was going back to Oldham where I would probably never get a game again. Plus, with just a few hours left of the transfer window, nobody else was going to come in for me at that late stage so I just said, 'I'm signing.'

Robert shrugged his shoulders. We drove back to Bolton where I collected one or two things, then it was back down the M6 to Solihull where I would meet club officials and sign a deal that would cost Blues about £225,000. That day, Birmingham signed myself, Andy Saville, George Parris, Scott Hiley, David Smith, Richard Dryden and Bob Catlin – the magnificent seven!

I'd signed on Thursday evening, had dinner at the hotel where we were all staying for the night and the following morning, the gaffer came to see us at breakfast and said, 'I know you're all sat here and it's a bit of an unusual situation with seven lads all signing at once on the same day, but I want to quell any questions or thoughts you might be having and just tell you you're all on the same money.'

And we were. It was about £1,000 per week, but it was unreal he'd had the foresight to think that way because it would have become a massive elephant in the room. Then it was off to training to start preparing for the first game.

We were all pitched in straight away in the match a few days later, but it was a bit of a nightmare because none of us knew each other that well or how each other played. In all honesty, we barely knew each other's names.

We had 13 games to turn things around, but we'd lost the first of them 1-0 to Bristol City and got booed off by an expectant crowd that was about 5,000 more than the average St Andrew's gate had been that season. It wasn't the best way to begin our careers with the club. We also felt we'd let down the owner, David Sullivan, who had taken the club out of administration by paying £700,000 and had installed Karren Brady as his managing director, aged 23. They were all pulling to get the club out of the mess we were in, but we'd lost that first game and it didn't feel good.

The following Monday, all six of the new signings present (only the keeper Bob Catlin didn't go with us) left the five-star hotel we'd been staying at in the city centre and were all rehoused at a guest house in Acocks Green.

It was a large Victorian house that had several other residents, including railway workers, salesmen and businessmen – and it was run by a guy called Simon. We all looked at each other as we walked in and it was a bit like, 'What the fuck are we doing here?' – but it turned out to be the best thing that ever happened because the camaraderie and bond that it helped us form was fantastic for all of us and for the club. We got to know each other, we ate, drank, and travelled together and pretty quickly that filtered into the rest of the squad and the football we played on the pitch.

It was at Birmingham that I crossed paths again with my old mate Jason Beckford. He'd had a bad knee injury and had bulked up top while he made his recovery. He was on a machine that bent his knee for 14 hours while lying on a bed and as soon as he saw me walk through the door, he had a beaming smile. We were able to rekindle what had been a great friendship at Manchester City.

John Frain was the club captain and was a dyed-in-the-wool Birmingham fan since childhood having been born in the city. He was a fantastic leader and the perfect skipper, who knew how to get the best out of all of us.

In the next 12 games, we somehow managed to turn it around, winning five, drawing four and losing three. And three matches in, I met an old 'friend' as we played Barnsley at home – they were now managed by Mel Machin. I didn't realise he was manager there, but Andy Saville came up to me before the game and said, 'We've got to get it on today, this one's for him.' I asked who he meant, and he said he was talking about Machin. Saville had been at Barnsley and Machin treated him exactly the same as he'd treated me.

You'd get a game, score, but then be dropped when injured players came back after a couple of games. He had messed with his head just as he had with mine and Andy Saville was a great centre-forward.

It was an added incentive for us both that night. We won 3-0 and I don't think either Andy or I could have played any better. As I ran off down the tunnel at full time, I saw Machin and smacked his cap off his head as I passed him. As he bent over to pick it up, he got a boot up the arse as well. My money is on Andy Saville for that one!

After the game, Machin came into our dressing room and said, 'Terry, can I have a word? Something happened out there, and I want two of your players reprimanded.'

He was fuming, but Terry said, 'Yeah I'll be out in a moment.' He ended up just glossing over it and told Machin he would deal with it. It felt good to have pissed him off, even if it was only a minor bit of payback.

Another of those run-in games was a bizarre home defeat to Swindon Town on Easter Monday. They had Glenn Hoddle and Micky Hazard playing for them and were different class on that day, but after I scored one and Saville made it 4-1, we switched off and thought we'd won it. Then they scored five goals to win 6-4. After the game, Cooper came in and we thought he'd tear a strip off us, but instead he said, 'We could have done with a win, lads, but if we keep playing football like that, the crowds will flock back. Fuck me, what a great game to be involved in even though we lost. Toe to toe with one of the best teams in the league – if we keep playing like that, we'll be fine and stay up.'

It was one of the most enjoyable games I'd ever played in from a pure footballing point of view, and afterwards in the players' lounge I met my dad. He and my mum had bought a chippy in Bolton a year or two before, so he didn't get to see many games anymore, but he said, 'You're starting to look like a player now. Excellent, well done.'

I had to smile as I was 25 years old and I think it was the first praise he'd ever given me because it had always been a case of, 'You did OK, but what can we improve on?'

The last of those 12 games was at home to Charlton Athletic at St Andrew's in front of more than 22,000 Bluenoses. We'd clawed back the points deficit and knew that a win would mean we stayed up. I was lucky enough to score the only goal of the game in a 1-0 win.

I'd played in all 13 games and scored five goals and had loved every minute of it. I felt like I was back in town, as Derek Sutton might have said.

It had been a huge effort by all the lads, that made national news because the situation had looked so hopeless. On a personal level, I'd rolled the dice and for once they'd come up in my favour – I could have been going into the following season as a third-tier footballer, but now everything in the garden looked rosy, and I suppose that should have set the alarm bells ringing given the number of false dawns I'd had.

The Monday after the Charlton game, there was a kit shoot at St Andrew's. I'd travelled back to Bolton on the Sunday to see family and friends and I asked my grandad if he wanted a ride out to Birmingham with me to have a look around. He said, 'Yeah, that'd be good, but we'll have to stop on the way for the toilet.'

We arrived at the ground and everyone at the club was still cock-a-hoop about staying up. All of us as players, we felt like the kings of Birmingham. I took my grandad down to the pitch and asked if he wanted to have a walk on the grass. So we had a stroll into the middle and I heard a voice shout, 'Get off the pitch you little fucker!'

It was the groundsman, so my grandad started to panic a bit, but I told him it was fine and that he was just pulling our leg. He came running round with a big smile and said, 'Paul – what about Saturday?' He thought my grandad was my dad and said, 'Was it you who taught him to score goals like that?'

My grandad smiled but shook his head and said it wasn't – but it was. I'd spent more time with him as a kid because my dad was working and also playing as a semi-pro at the time, and it was he who showed me various finishing techniques and got me to practise them endlessly.

I said, 'Don't take that humble approach, grandad – it was you.' My grandad was so made up – first that we weren't getting a bollocking for being on the pitch and secondly because somebody thought so much about his grandson. Karren Brady came down to say hello and was ever so polite and respectful towards him, but I wouldn't have expected anything less from her. It was a lovely few hours and it meant so much to him.

I saw Karren a bit later in the canteen, where she took me back a bit when she told me Serie A side Pisa had enquired about the possibility of signing me and Andy Saville. It was completely out of the blue, but Andy had two kids and didn't really fancy moving abroad. Did I want to leave Birmingham? No, not at all, but the chance of playing in Italy for two or three years would have been interesting. Karren told me after that conversation that we were going to Italy for pre-season anyway, so I thought I'd see what panned out.

We did the kit shoot and I headed back to Bolton with my grandad, who looked pleased as punch. He said, 'It all seems to be slipping into place for you now – all you have to do is stay fit.'

I said, 'Yeah, that's right grandad.'

He smiled all the way back to Bolton and just looked happy and content and I was glad I'd been able to spend a few quality hours in his company.

I went away with the lads to Tenerife for a week, came home and had another couple of weeks away with Clare, my long-term girlfriend, before starting to do the odd bits and bobs as pre-season started to loom on the horizon. I started doing 12 minutes on the bike with my dad running, and then we'd swap over, I'd run, and he'd cycle for 12 minutes and so on as I started to build my sharpness back up. I wanted to be as fit as possible by the time I went back to the club, and I felt the best I'd ever felt by the time we started pre-season.

One of the early sessions was to get a partner and carry them on your back. Richard Dryden made a beeline for me and said he'd put me on his back first. He lifted me up and said, in his best West Country accent, 'Fuck me! How heavy are you? I only picked you because you're one of the smallest here. Fucking hell, man!'

I told him it was all muscle, and I wasn't far wrong. He was 6ft 2in and then I had to carry him around on my back like a goon for a few minutes before we started some 12-minute runs, and I was absolutely flying. I passed Richard and said, 'Keep up, Rich!' He laughed and said, 'Fucking hell – I didn't think you were fit, neither!'

Louie Donowa was an athletic lad, but I smashed him and was just flying that first week of training. Then we set off for Italy where we'd play a couple of friendlies. Before we flew out, Trevor Morgan pulled everyone together and told us all there would be no drinking on the trip. When we got to Italy the coach wasn't there on time, so we were hanging around in the terminal and Trevor relented and, without much persuasion, said, 'Let's get a round in!'

We were meant to train mid-afternoon, but the gaffer said it was too hot and we'd have a session the following morning instead when it was cooler.

We got up early before the sun started cracking the flags and, as we had a game the following day, Cooper said, 'It's just a light session – nothing strenuous with a bit of shadow play and that'll do for today.' It was 7am and it was already red-hot, and we were to have a game between the lads who were starting the match the next day and the rest of the squad. Gianni Paladini had some association with Birmingham at the time and was an agent of some sort who was always offering players and trialists. He would eventually become the chairman of QPR, but on this occasion he'd brought an Argentinian defender who, unbeknown to us, didn't speak a word of English and he was lining up against me. He was a big lad – maybe 6ft 4in. Terry told us we were just playing a shadow game – so no tackling, just run through a few corners and free kicks for the game the following day. I kicked the game off with Andy Saville, all relaxed – 11 versus six – a nice easy morning just running through things, or so I thought.

Next thing, Scott Hiley played the ball to me, I let it run, turned and this Argentinian guy absolutely clattered into me from nowhere with a sliding tackle. The force he hit me with detached three ligaments from my ankle and that was my pre-season over.

I was back to square one again and all because this lad didn't understand English! I was completely gutted that it had happened again, especially after I'd worked so hard and felt so good. I went for an X-ray in Italy where the scans confirmed the detached ligaments. Karren wanted me to stay on tour for some reason, but I needed to get home. My surgeon, Tony Banks, was away on holiday so I couldn't get the operation I needed straight away anyway. It was like a recurring nightmare. But something else was to happen on this trip that was an even bigger blow for me. The phone rang in my hotel room. It was my dad and he said, 'Are you sitting down, lad?' I sort of half laughed and asked why I needed to sit down. He said to just take a seat for a minute. I did and then he told me to brace myself and he told me my grandad had just passed away.

He had died on the bowling green, doing what he liked best, and just went out like a light when he went down to pick one of his bowls up. That was that. If he could have chosen a way to go, that would have probably been it, and it was bittersweet in many ways because we'd had that lovely day together and he'd been so happy. I'd had the chance to tell him what an influence he'd been on my career, and he'd seen me playing at somewhere close to my best.

He was such a great bloke, and it goes without saying I loved him to bits and would miss him forever. To say it had been a rough few days for me was something of an understatement and I just wanted to get my ankle sorted and get my mind back on football so I could focus on something else.

19

Same Old, Same Old

TONY BANKS stuck the ligaments back to my ankle, but it took a bit longer than we'd hoped to recover as I kept getting a nipping feeling that wouldn't settle down. Banksy – as he was now called on speed dial in my phone – was going to go back in and have a look but he decided not to in the end and I started having a bit of physio instead with Mandy Johnson, who was one of the first female sports physiotherapists at a football club in the country. She was shit-hot at her job, too.

I missed all pre-season and would be out until late November, when I was finally declared fit to play, against Tranmere Rovers. I'd been out almost six months by that point and Birmingham hadn't been able to carry the momentum of the previous season into 1993/94. We'd won four, drawn five and lost seven, but we were going into the Tranmere match on the back of three straight defeats.

In the days before the game, I went to see the physio and told him I had a bit of tightness in my Achilles tendon, so he advised me to do some gentle stretching exercises and told me I should be fine. By Friday morning I could hardly walk, but I was so pissed off that I continued with the stretches because there was no way I was going to say I couldn't play the next day.

By Saturday the pain was even worse, but I did some stretches again, the physio gave me a massage and told me to just get through this 90 minutes and then they'd investigate what the cause was. I started the game and at half-time I just put my trainers on and kept walking up and down the tunnel, so the stiffness didn't set in again, then put my boots on and went out. I played OK – not fantastic – but we got hammered 3-0 and there were a few rumblings among the supporters and a couple of 'Cooper out!' chants.

We went back into the dressing room and Terry Cooper sat us down and said, 'Look lads, we did ever so well last season and I love working with you all, but I'm not having that. I don't need this job. I'm not having my missus slagged off at the supermarket, so that's it. I'm off.' He then went upstairs and handed his resignation into David Sullivan just like that. Karren Brady came down shortly after to confirm Terry had quit.

That left us without a manager for the time being and Karren sort of took the reins in the interim and told us we were all to come in the next day, a Sunday, for a training and running session. I tried to take part in the running we began with, but every step I took it felt like somebody was stabbing me in the back of my heel with a knife. She insisted I continue so I limped around, but the atmosphere at the club was, by now, toxic.

The following Tuesday, a practice match was organised between the first 11 who started against Tranmere and our reserve team, with Trevor Morgan refereeing. Karren appeared from nowhere and told Trevor she would be refereeing the game. It wasn't your average training session, that was for sure.

Jason Beckford was back in training by that point and, before the game began, Karren asked him to go and change the scoreboard which said 'Blues 0-3 Visitors'. At Birmingham back then, they used to have a guy in white overalls who used to climb up a house ladder and change the scoreboard – all high-tech stuff!

'Go and take it down, Jason,' Karren said, and she started the game. Jason sauntered over towards the scoreboard and stopped a few feet short, then looked up and down at it three or four times before turning back around and going to sit on the bench.

'I've told you to change that scoreboard, Jason,' Karren shouted over. She stopped the game and came over and asked Jason why he hadn't changed it.

Jason said, 'There's nothing in my contract that says I have to change scoreboards.'

'I won't task you again, Jason. Now go and change it!' she said.

But Jason was adamant he wasn't changing it and he told her so.

In a scene that was a snapshot into Karren's future TV career on *The Apprentice*, she said, 'That's it. Jason, you're fired. Go and get your gear and I'll call you later. Be by your phone this afternoon. You can't talk to me like that.'

It was a pivotal moment for Karren, who knew that if she backed down then nobody would take anything she said seriously.

Jason later contacted the PFA, but as predictable as ever they just agreed that he couldn't talk to his boss that way and that was the end of that. What a shame. He was probably just in the wrong place at the wrong time with everything falling apart around us, and also like I had been at Oldham, he was coming back from one of the worst injuries I'd personally ever known a footballer to have.

Meanwhile, I went back to see Tony Banks to try and figure out what the problem was and after several scans of the area that had been giving me excruciating pain, he discovered a cyst on my Achilles tendon – a proper nightmare scenario for any footballer.

My injury was discussed and managed by Karren, Tony and Mandy Johnson and everyone was kept in the loop while we tried to get me back playing again, and in the interim, Barry Fry became our new manager.

I hadn't had chance to chat with him yet so at the club's Christmas party in early December, I saw him for the first time and went over and said, 'Can I have a quiet word with you?' He said, 'Not now, but next week, yeah.'

I was having my operation the next day and had wanted to let him know what was happening, but he never gave me the chance. I stayed for a couple of hours, didn't drink, and then drove back to Bolton and, in the morning, went into hospital where Tony removed the cyst. He told me I'd need two weeks in plaster, two weeks under the care of Mandy Johnson and the rehab would need to be spot on.

I did exactly what they told me and I was ready to return to Birmingham after a month of recovery to start running again, but before I could, I got a call from a local journo saying I should get my arse down there because everything was about to kick off.

I'd been working my bollocks off and done as much as I could – weights, swimming and cycling – and then I found out Barry Fry had given an interview to the *Birmingham Mail* with a picture of me saying 'Paul Moulden: Wanted Dead or Alive', claiming he hadn't seen me in the six weeks he'd been manager at St Andrew's.

I couldn't believe it. I couldn't have worked any harder to get back, and to be returning after four weeks following an Achilles op was almost unheard of, and now Fry was effectively telling the fans that I was somebody who didn't give a toss about the club or my own career. I was so angry; every bit of my rehab had been documented and the paperwork was right there in Karren's office for him to see if he'd taken the trouble to ask – but he hadn't and decided to throw me under the bus instead.

I saw Karren a bit later and told her what was going on and she said, 'Oh, you know what he's like.' What bothered me was that Fry was tarnishing my name when I was doing everything I could to get back, partly I think to deflect from his poor start at the club.

There were 46 professional players at Birmingham City at the time – 46 – and I quickly realised I was way down the pecking order. From the brilliance of Terry Cooper's man-management to this clown. That's the life of a footballer sometimes, but it felt like I'd run over a bag of black cats because whenever I climbed back up off the canvas, I was floored again with a right hook from out of nowhere.

By the end of that season, I'd started just seven games and not scored once. In hindsight, I realise at that time I was starting to clutch at straws. I wanted my career to carry on and regenerate, but it felt like it was a losing battle. I'd been out for eight months at Manchester City with a shin injury, then a broken back, then at Oldham I'd spent the best part of nine months out with my ankle, at Birmingham I'd had another six months out with my detached ankle ligaments and more time out with my Achilles operation. That's a huge amount of time out and the injuries had each taken their toll, slowed me down and my fitness had suffered accordingly. Four major injuries, not to mention my three broken legs as a teenager. I was 27 and for the first time I was wondering if I had the stomach to do it all again.

My old mate from Bournemouth – Shaun Brooks – said Andy Saville and myself should both have a listen to Stockport County where he was now based if we were looking to move on. There was nothing to lose, so we went up and spoke to the manager Danny Bergara, who had put a bid in for both of us, and I honestly think we could have worked wonders there but his offer was £225 per week each. We were on £1,000 at Birmingham. It was a pittance in comparison and I'm certain I could have earned more at Tesco. Andy said it wouldn't even cover his petrol, so I had a word with Shaun because I thought Danny was taking the piss, but he confirmed that was the same money he was on, with the promise of more if they got promoted.

We turned it down as it just didn't make financial sense and Danny gave an interview in the *Manchester Evening News* a day or so later saying, 'Moulden and Saville want turkey breast, but I can only offer chicken legs.'

To say I was becoming a little cynical towards the game by that stage was a slight understatement.

I went back to Birmingham, spoke with Karren, and just asked if the club could release me. We'd been sold this dream of pulling together to get Birmingham out of a mess, I worked hard and went above and beyond, but everything had changed since Fry's arrival. There was no future for me there and it just made sense all round for me to be let go.

I was still a Birmingham player by the start of the 1994/95 pre-season and I played in a friendly against Stevenage, scoring a couple of times and performing well.

By then, we had three teams of senior players, with the third team – the one I was in – being the best of the lot because it had all the players Terry Cooper had signed. Our next game was a friendly against Leicester, so I went into the first-team dressing room and the coaches in there said, 'Oh, think you did well against Stevenage? You're a first-team player are you now?' They were having a bit of a laugh, and I was laughing with them having a bit of banter and said, 'With this fucker, you never know, do you?'

Then Fry walked in and said, 'What are you doing in here?' I told him I thought I'd done well enough to play against Leicester, but I could see there was no chance so I walked out. Martin O'Neill, managing Leicester, was passing and said, 'What's going on in there?'

I said, 'Ah, it's just my boss being a dick.'

Fry was right behind me and said, 'You fucking what?!'

That was the end for me at Birmingham and I knew it. I went to see Karren and David Sullivan again and though they dragged it out a bit, they eventually agreed I could be released from my contract. I was paid up and that was that. I think there were only five months or so left on my contract, so it wasn't a major severance.

Danny Wallace left the same day and Fry came over before we left, swept Danny's cap off and put the cheque under it. Then he said to me that a club in the Isthmian League wanted to sign me, and he was like a different character, but I'd had my fill of him so I just walked out and left Birmingham City behind once and for all; it was like leaving Manchester City all over again because I loved the place.

As a footnote to my time with the Blues, there was a moment I remember that didn't seem to have much significance at the time, but in the years that would follow, it definitely did. Danny and I both went in to see the physio at the same time, and both of us had the same complaint – lower back pain.

The physio examined us and came to the same conclusion for both Danny and me – we were doing too much driving and his solution was that we each buy a house in Birmingham.

I had no clue that it was actually the start of a long-term hip issue for me, but Danny's was much more serious as that had been the first signs of multiple sclerosis.

So, buying a house in Birmingham wouldn't have cured either of our issues.

20
The Wanderer

MY PHONE could best be described as 'warm' after I left Birmingham City. The two most appealing offers were short-term contracts at Grimsby Town, managed by Brian Laws, and Huddersfield Town, then under the guidance of Neil Warnock.

I was quite impressed with Laws but the thought of living in digs again didn't appeal, while Huddersfield was a 40-minute drive from Bolton so I decided to take their offer of a three-month deal.

I'd be mainly injury and suspension cover for Andy Booth and Ronnie Jepson, who were having a great season and had got around 50 goals between them at that point, so I knew I would have limited chances, but they were going well in the Second Division and I was happy with their offer. If I got a few games under my belt, so much the better.

Before I agreed, I spoke with people who had played under Warnock before and they all had good words to say about him.

When I met him, I have to admit I found him a decent guy. My condition was good but I was lacking in match fitness as I'd only been playing representative games for Birmingham before I left – glorified friendlies against all kinds of teams – which was all OK, but nothing like the real thing.

Huddersfield had a reserve team in the Pontins League (formerly the Central League), so I figured I'd get at least one competitive game a week with the reserves if nothing else.

It turned out to be an up and down time in many ways because you never quite knew where you were with Warnock – and that wasn't just my opinion – it applied to everyone at the club, bar maybe Ronnie Jepson. He'd be all right one minute and not that great the next, but that was management and that's just how he was.

One moment I remember was when I was down to be sub in one game and I came in to get changed on matchday but another lad was getting changed in my spot in the dressing room. I asked what he was doing, and he said, 'Getting changed for the game.' I told him to look at the team sheet, so he did and saw his name wasn't there. 'Fuck me,' he said and started to get changed again as quickly as he could. But he wasn't quick enough. Warnock walked in and we all took a deep breath, wondering if he'd give this lad a bollocking. Instead, Warnock asked why he was there and he said, 'I thought I was playing, gaffer, I'm going to get changed now.'

Warnock said, 'No, don't. I'm superstitious – keep your kit on; Mouldy – fuck off and go sit in the stands and watch!' Charming!

Another morning we all arrived for training and were told we had to drink sherry and raw eggs, supposedly to help build us up, but I couldn't stomach it and spewed up everywhere, much to everyone's amusement. I was thinking, 'What the fuck is this all about?' Huddersfield was a strange place to be, if I'm honest, and I ended up playing a couple of sub appearances without scoring and not much else. Huddersfield got to the play-offs and beat Bristol Rovers in the final to go up to what is now the Championship, so everyone was cock-a-hoop.

I travelled back from Wembley with the team, but that was my time there done. My contract was up and I was looking for a club once again. There was never going to be an extension at Huddersfield, and if I'm totally honest I wouldn't have wanted one. They'd filled a gap at the end of the 1994/95 season and I'd been training and playing reserves games so I was happy enough with the whole scenario, which had worked for the club and for me. Could it have been better? Of course it could, but I was at a point where beggars couldn't be choosers and, if nothing else, I've always been a realist. Now, almost aged 28, I just needed to find somewhere I could have a pre-season with, prove myself and hopefully get a contract. I sat down with my adviser Robert Campbell (probably only Paul Gascoigne had an agent back then so advisers were as near as you got to representation) and we identified several clubs I thought I might have a chance with, so he then sent off letters to them all. If it all seems like a different world to today, that's because it was.

I went on holiday, expecting my answering machine to be full on my return – but I didn't have one single message. It was a reality check I could have done without, but it was reflective of where I was at. I had to start ringing around myself to try and find a club. I'd had a good summer, I had been running with Robbie Brightwell and been on the weights with Tony Banks and I felt as fit as a butcher's dog. The only issue was my ankle, which was still sore most of the time, but that was something I was going to have to live with.

Stockport County said I was welcome to spend the pre-season with them. Dave Jones was now in charge, and it was good. I enjoyed it, but I think they looked at my past history, probably thought I'd had a lot of knocks and with the small budget they were working with, I'm pretty sure they thought they couldn't take a gamble on me.

The free transfer list circulated by the FA had now been sent to clubs across the land, naming every player who was available, and things were finally starting to happen. My old team-mate from Manchester City, Nicky Reid, who was now a physio at Wigan Athletic, called me and said I should go and train with them so I was only too happy to do so. My first session was to be on a Thursday, but two nights before that I got a call from one of the directors at Torquay United asking whether I fancied playing in a game against a touring Jamaica side because Wally Downes – who had worked at Bournemouth – had recommended me. I said I would, but first I had to train with Wigan because it looked like there might be a chance of me signing for them.

Training for Wigan and playing for Torquay both in the same day was madness, even though I felt fit enough to carry it off, but the session with Wigan was longer than I'd anticipated and I didn't get away until 1.30pm. Then it was straight on to the M6 and then M5 for the 270-odd mile drive to Torquay. I bombed it there, but it still took nearly five hours and when I arrived, I got a bollocking for being late. The guy who was taking the game said, 'Do you want to play for this football club or not?'

I thought about telling him to shove it up his arse, but instead smiled and just said, 'To be honest mate, I trained with Wigan this morning and then headed straight down here.' I got changed, but we went out and the last thing I needed was a lesson in football because Jamaica knocked it around us for fun and we barely got a kick. They were fantastic to watch, which is pretty much all we did!

It had been a team of trialists I'd played in, with Torquay taking the chance to check out the free agents they were looking at for their starting XI. I went back into the dressing room, looked around and thought, 'What the fuck am I doing here?' I wasn't getting paid, had bust a gut to get to Torquay and for what? The Torquay coach tried to tear a strip off a few of the lads, who were all there just to try and win a contract or have a chance and I was very much of the 'Nah, I'm not having you, pal' mindset. I got changed, and in the car park one of the directors came across, smiled, and said, 'Here's something towards your petrol,' and put a tenner in my top pocket! Jesus – had I slipped that far down the ladder? I got in the car and headed for the seafront where I bought two lots of fish and chips before setting off for Bolton.

As for my career, I wondered where, if anywhere, I was headed. I'd worked hard to get fit all summer and, at 28, I should have been at the peak of my powers, but the truth was I was nearing the end of the road and episodes like Torquay demonstrated exactly how far off the radar I had drifted.

Nothing came of my sessions with Wigan, but in between I had spoken to Rochdale manager Mick Docherty a few times and as it was only 30 minutes from home, I thought, 'Why not?' If I could get a few reserve games and build up my match fitness, it would be worthwhile. I'd be playing at a few football outposts, but it was something I was prepared to do.

The training was OK, but the standard in the reserve league they were in was awful and I probably scored 17 goals in five games – it was ridiculous, and I was much better than that. I was there playing for free, but I felt like a nomad with no direction or future. Then the first team had a League Cup game against Darlington and I didn't have to go and watch if I didn't fancy it, but I wanted to as I had nothing better to do, so I went home, had some dinner – thankfully, no dessert – and headed back to Spotland.

When I arrived, the gaffer was waiting at the door. He said, 'Have you brought your boots with you?' As it turned out, they were still in my car, so I said I had and he said, 'Right, let's get you signed up – you're playing tonight.' I had to sign a form that effectively registered me for Rochdale – I suppose you could call it a 'guest' – but as a non-contract player, so I played in the game and ended up scoring a perfect hat-trick. Right foot, left foot and a header! I'd been pushed from pillar to post, but this was one of the most satisfying moments of my career because, in spite of everything, I'd proved that if I was given the opportunity, I knew where the back of the net was.

Afterwards, the gaffer told me the chairman wanted a word with me the next day. I came in and he offered me a year's contract which worked for me, and I spent that season with Rochdale on £500 per week. The first few months were great but my ankle was getting worse as time went on. The fact Rochdale didn't have a physio helped me conclude that my ankle was actually never going to be right and most likely my career was over. I did my best for them and saw the season out, but when they had a meeting over new contracts at the end of the campaign I just told them the truth – I wasn't fit for anything, and I couldn't train full time anymore. They thanked me for my efforts, the chairman gave me two FA Cup Final tickets, and that was the end of that.

I didn't want to be on the scrapheap at 29, but all the injuries had taken their toll and I knew that, no matter what, my ankle was never going to get any better. I thought about all the times in my career where I'd been to see the physio with a hamstring pull, calf strain or some other minor soft-tissue injury – and there had been virtually none. It had always been a broken leg, a broken ankle, a broken back, a hernia, AChilles tendons detached; I would have loved to have had a thigh strain at some point! It was never a case of 'don't worry, you'll be back in five or six weeks' – it was always six to eight months for me.

I'd managed my ankle as best I could, but it had always been a case of when one door closed, another one slammed in my face. I was at the end of the road, and I didn't have a clue what I was going to do. The only way I can explain how I was feeling was that it was similar to when you are given homework over Christmas and you don't do it – and then the night before you're back to school, you think, 'Actually, I should have done this.'

I was the kid who never did his homework. I didn't know what I was going to do next because football had been everything to me and I'd never really thought of what came next. Clare was now my wife, she was also pregnant with our first child, and I was wondering how I would be able to provide for them and put food on the table.

To say it was a scary time is an understatement.

21

Frying by the Seat of My Pants

SO, WHAT next?

I spent a few weeks talking to my dad, trying to figure out what the best direction to go in was. He thought I might be able to find somewhere I could train part-time if my ankle wasn't up to more than that and then I got a call from Trevor Morgan, my old coach at Birmingham who was now in Australia. He asked if I fancied playing in the A-League for a while and, though it initially seemed appealing, my mum had probably heard enough. She said I'd be heavily taxed if I went there and having experienced Norway and how expensive it was to live there, she had a point when she said I'd be barely breaking even. Besides, wasn't I just delaying the inevitable?

It was a long way to go to find that out and she said that I had to think of football as my former life now and get my act together. And, of course, she was spot on. It *was* my former life, but actually getting your head around that isn't that easy.

I was missing my grandad a lot because he was another one who never wrapped anything up in cotton wool. I remembered that time he'd told me that everything was going my way at that point when I was scoring goals for fun and doing really well for England Schoolboys. He said that 65 to 70 per cent of football was about disappointment. Of course, he meant more along the lines of you win, you lose, you fall out with managers, you get dropped – not what actually happened to me in terms of injuries, but in his own way he was absolutely right.

It was time to put football on the back burner and focus on earning a living. My first son, Joe, had been born and I had responsibilities to pay the mortgage and feed him and my wife.

Mum and Dad asked me why I hadn't thought about getting a chip shop. They'd done well running theirs for the last five or six years and I'd helped them out over that time and I knew enough about what they did to have a head start, so I said I would give it some thought.

Eventually, I thought I'd give it a go. I decided to buy a chip shop that had been struggling in Great Lever, a few miles away from Mum and Dad, on the understanding that if I didn't like it or manage to turn it around, they'd come and buy it off me. In that respect, I couldn't really lose.

We decided it would be like a franchise of Tony and Brenda's chippy – called Paul's Chippy – so primarily I'd do everything they did in their shop, with the same potatoes, oil, fish, pies, curry and gravy, plus the same prices. And that's what we did.

The shop I bought was a real tip – just awful – so the first week I got it, I was still training with Tony Banks at Wythenshawe and my mate Nicky Spooner, who was still playing for Bolton Wanderers. Nicky came back to the shop with me. He looked around and just said, 'What the hell have you bought? I hope you know what you're doing.'

It made me wonder for a bit and, at first, I thought he was right – it was a mess – but I truly believed I could pull it off. One thing I'd learned from my mum and dad was that for every £1 you earned, you had to spend 25p of it on the shop and, eventually, you would turn it around. My dad said it wasn't the condition of the shop, more the quality of the food that you were serving that would get the punters in, so I felt like Nicky had thrown down a gauntlet. He hadn't because it had just been an observation, but it made me think, 'Right, if I'm doing this, I'm going to be the best I can possibly be at this game. I'll smash this and eventually I'll be as good as anybody running a chippy.'

I worked hard and steadily, word got around that what we were doing was good. About eight months in, a guy came to service the range and told me I needed bigger burners because the recovery time wasn't quick enough, so when the chips were fried they weren't being kept warm enough in the storage compartment. He said he knew how to fix it, so he changed the burners to give everything more oomph and went on his way.

A few days after that the shop burned down! Three fire engines came, but the place was gutted, as was I. What the fuck?

Three people turned up from the insurance company one morning, two in suits and one in jeans and a T-shirt. They were examining this and that and I had a quiet word with the guy in jeans – his name turned out to be Dave Drinkwater – and I'll never forget his response when I asked him who he was. He said, 'I'm the fucker that's going to resurrect this shop so shut up and listen.'

It turned out Dave knew his stuff and he figured out that the guy who had serviced the machinery had made the burners too hot. They then ignited a lump of fat and started the fire that had all but destroyed the shop. My insurers and the servicer's insurers met, agreed the liability lay with the servicing I'd had and as a result the shop had a £24,000 overhaul. New floors, new ceilings, new cooker – everything was brand new. It turned out I'd had a bit of luck and the shop Nicky had seen was unrecognisable – suddenly, we were well on our way!

Along with a lady called Liz Greenhalgh, who had worked in chip shops all over Bolton, we went around various chippies that had good reputations. They were happy to pass on their tips and advice, all so we could be the best we could be.

During this transition from footballer to chip-shop owner, I crossed paths with Brent Peters, who was a big fish (pardon the pun) in non-league football. Brent was a footballing director at Accrington Stanley and around June or early July, he called me and asked if I would play for Accrington. He arranged to come and see me in the shop, and I just explained that my ankle was too sore to play.

He asked me why I didn't just train once a week and play every Saturday. In truth, I was still desperate to play so I told my dad who said, 'Well, you're still the same as you were when you were 18 or 19 so you could do that, couldn't you? Give it a go.' And I did.

Accrington covered my petrol money, so I signed a deal. They were managed by a Scouser called Eric Whalley, a great guy who I really got on with. I coped OK with pre-season, played in a few friendlies and he understood the situation I was in. He could see the state of my ankle after each game, which was often twice the size of the other one.

But they changed managers before the start of the season, and one thing I'd found in general was that the lower down the football ladder I went, the worse the managers were. They thought they were great, but they weren't. I still had my mum's words echoing around my head about football being my former life and that I needed to focus on running my business.

Not long afterwards, I was at the fish market at stupid o'clock in the morning as I was every day when the shop was open – I had to, or else I'd have no fish to sell – and there would be people there from restaurants, shops and other chippies. There were about 30 people there this particular day and someone shouted over, 'You all right, has-been?' It was a larger-than-life character I knew from Bolton called Trevor Barber, so I just laughed and asked him how he was doing. He was just having a bit of banter, which I always enjoyed.

When I'd chosen my fish and went to pay, the cashier – a guy I was starting to get to know reasonably well – said, 'Cheeky bastard. I'll have a word with him later.' But I told him I was fine with it and at the end of the day the guy was right. I was a has-been when it came to football. It made me think along the lines of, 'What am I actually doing?' Signing for Accrington was nuts, I didn't have the time and my ankle wouldn't stand up to it, so I phoned Brent, thanked him for everything but told him I couldn't play for his club anymore, or any other come to that. He told me he'd seen me play and that I'd done well, but I just said, 'Brent, I'm just kidding myself. My focus needs to be on what I'm doing now.'

And it did – as a result, the shop was soon doing really well. I got my head down and focused on my new life. But fast forward another eight months and Brent called me again. He'd bought Bacup Borough in the North West Counties League Division Two and was doing everything – manager, owner and chairman! He wanted to know if I wanted to come and play for his new club. I told him I hadn't even trained for eight months, but it's almost impossible to say no to Brent Peters. My ankle had got a bit easier, and he said I just had to play on Saturdays with no training needed, plus my dad had played for Bacup, which meant there was a sort of connection already there, so I accepted the offer.

It meant me getting back on my bike and getting as fit as I could, but it just about worked for everyone, and I ended up playing for Bacup Borough for four years, and you know what? I really enjoyed it. I suggested a couple of lads who might help the club, so they started coming along, which was great. I moved back a bit when I played – the number ten role, or lazy midfielder as it was known back then – and I loved it. I was playing with mates, managing my ankle, and playing football again, with the odd goal thrown in here and there.

I had some great times at Bacup, and it couldn't have fitted better into my working life. Every Saturday, I'd work at the chippy at lunchtime and head off to play football for Brent. I was earning money from the shop and I could still play football, so in many ways it was perfect.

One time, away to Great Harwood, I got there seven minutes before kick-off and Brent was sat there with the rest of the lads as cool as you like and just said, 'I knew you'd get here, it's not a problem. If you were late, we'd have started with ten players. When we have 11, we're unbeaten and near the top of the league. It's not a problem.'

Another time, he called me up on Saturday morning and said, 'I can't fucking believe it, I can't fucking believe it.' I asked him what was up, and he said, 'Fleetwood Town have got seven days on you, and you can't play today.'

To explain, when a club puts seven days on you, it is sort of an official request to speak with you. In effect, the deal with Bacup meant I wasn't tied to anyone because I was an on-contract player and therefore not a professional – it gives a club seven days to approach and talk with you, but it also means you can't play for anyone else.

Fleetwood had reformed, had money behind them and had some momentum, but my ankle was a mess after every game I played so I didn't think there was any mileage in it. I told Brent to get the Fleetwood guy to give me a ring so I could sort it out.

This guy tried to sell the project to me and told me the club was going places. If I'm honest, I wanted to be part of it. They told me they'd been watching me and, even at 34, they thought I could still do it, so would I be interested in playing for them? Of course, I was, but there was no way I actually could.

He told me they trained Tuesday and Thursday and I stopped him there and said, 'Woah, wait a minute – I don't train, and I just play on a Saturday.'

They were offering decent money and he told me they'd expect me to train twice a week and play matches as and when and I tried to explain that just wasn't going to happen. The shop's success meant that we now had our fish delivered and a few of the guys I bought off came from Fleetwood so I'd asked how long it took to get to me. They both said an hour and 20 minutes. I'd spoken to them before speaking to the club, but the guy from Fleetwood couldn't grasp what I was trying to say about the state of my ankle, my work and the limited time I had available. So, I changed it around and said, 'At Bacup, and it takes me 35 minutes to get there, I play for 90 minutes and then it's 35 minutes to get home. You want me to drive one hour and 20 minutes to train, then an hour and 20 to get home. Then do the same again two days later and then again on a Saturday. Why would I want to do that?'

I think the penny finally dropped, but credit to him and Fleetwood because they had the vision even back then in 1999/2000 and, today, they're a League One side who have had Joey Barton and Uwe Rösler as managers in recent years.

It might have been good for me and them, but my ankle just couldn't sustain that kind of intensity anymore.

Besides, I was more than happy to stay at Bacup. In some ways, I now had the best of both worlds. I had a thriving business with the chippy, and I was able to play football again, but on terms that were manageable time-wise, work-wise, and that fitted in with my family life.

We only had a handful of punters coming to watch us when we played at home, but Brent was such a nice guy you just wanted it to work for him.

I'd had a good run and extended my career by a few years but all good things come to an end. My last game ever was Bacup Borough v Castle St Gabriel's, and I was up against a young lad called Paul Lyons, who I'd been with at Rochdale. We went into a 50/50 challenge. Paul was about three stone soaking wet through and it was no more than a block tackle, but the impact span my knee around and, though it was a totally honest challenge, the day after I couldn't bend it or even walk on it, and I just thought that, had that been someone with a bit more beef behind them, it could have broken my leg and where would I have been then? I wouldn't have been able to work, drive or feed my family, so that was that.

It took me six or seven weeks to get right, my back was really sore, and I was 34 years old, playing for petrol money, and I thought, 'Fuck that.' I had a conversation with Brent, and, of course, he understood completely.

And that was the genuine end of my playing career. It was time to fully focus on what I *could* do over what I *wanted* to do. What I didn't know was that something worse than any broken bone I'd had would leave me literally hanging by a thread in the not-too-distant future.

22
Second Chance?

CLARE AND I had got married in December 1997 and Joe arrived in 1998. Ted was born in 2000 and Louie followed in 2002. Three boys and, by the time I was 37, they were running me ragged! They loved to play rugby in the back garden, but I'd been noticing more and more that the pain in my back was getting worse and I couldn't bend down to pick the ball up anymore.

When I was getting in my car, I had to almost pick my left leg up to get in. It was a crap second-hand car that we used to call the 'fish wagon' because I used it to pick up the fish in a morning, so it always stunk. I had a decent car for family life, but this old rust bucket was hard to get in and out of and, if I accidentally kicked the sill, the pain in my hips was excruciating. I was really down because of the pain – plus my ankle hurt like hell because I was stood up all day – so I finally went to see the doctor. After several scans, he told me it was my hip that was the problem, and I said it was just sore and must be something else. He said, 'No, Paul – it's your hip and it's goosed.'

He put me under the care of a consultant called Mr Porter because I was struggling with daily life and needed to be able to work and play with the kids. The doctor asked me how I might have damaged my hips and I told him I used to play a lot of football. He asked for who and I told him Manchester City.

'Really?' he said. 'I used to be a director at Everton. Whatever happened to that lad in the 1980s that scored a 25-yarder past Neville Southall at Maine Road?'

I said, 'Into the bottom corner?'

He nodded and said, 'Yeah, Neville Southall was the best keeper in the world and some whippersnapper buries a shot past him like that. I've never forgotten it.'

I told him he was talking to him.

He couldn't believe it!

He offered me the option of having both hips done at the same time, but I bottled it and said that one would do. As it was, within three years I needed the other one doing anyway because, once they'd straightened one side up, the other deteriorated soon after. I was aged 37 and then 40 when I had each one done.

I wish that had been the last time that I'd needed the help of medical professionals, but on 12 February 2002 I had an episode that could and probably should have meant I wouldn't be around to write this book.

It still gives me shudders.

At the time, I was running three football teams that my lads were involved in. There were other guys running them as well, but it meant we were playing Saturdays and Sundays and Joe, Ted and Louie were all doing ever so well which meant a logistical nightmare that I was front and centre of. I'd finish at the chippy at 2pm on weekdays and that's when friends would come to the shop to discuss this, that or the other, and then then phone would ring and I just didn't need the aggravation.

Joe's team reached the Lancashire Cup semi-final, and we battered the team we were playing, but we couldn't score, then a sub came on for the opposition late on, toe-bunged a shot over our keeper and we lost 1-0. The devastation was total, and it felt like we'd had a death in the family and the world was coming to an end at five o'clock. I can't explain what the disappointment felt like for Joe's team losing the way they did.

Two days later, a woman smashed into the back of my car at some traffic lights, and everything just seemed to come to a head over a very short period.

A week later, I'd finished a session at the chippy and I bent over to pick something up but I felt like I'd been smashed over the back of my head with a cricket bat, and I collapsed on to the tiles. As I lay there, a sickening wave came over me and I was suddenly freezing cold. I must have been there for about 40 to 50 minutes and I couldn't get up, and I remember thinking, 'This is it. I'm done for – and you know what? It's not so bad, is it?' It was quiet and surreal but a kind of peaceful feeling, but something inside me made me fight to get up.

I struggled to my feet and was unsteady but just about functional and managed to get out of the shop. As I did, a friend was passing. She told me to get to hospital because I looked so bad and that she knew someone who had not three months earlier died from a brain haemorrhage and suggested the same was happening to me. Great! Despite her advice, I instead got in my car and drove about 200 yards down the road to my mum's house. I walked in and she said, 'Paul, what's wrong with you?' I said I didn't have a clue and just kept asking her what time it was and it turned out it was around 3.15pm and Ted was due to have a trial at Manchester United after school and I knew I had to get him there.

I got back in the car, collected Ted and Louie from school and took them to The Cliff – God knows how – and when I got out the car, I stumbled a bit and felt dizzy. They both wanted me to go to hospital and because Salford Royal was close by, I decided I'd go and get checked over. It saved my life.

I parked the car, left the keys in there, walked straight into triage and told the nurse, 'I think I'm dying, love.' She told me to sit down, took a few details and then told me to just wait outside. I remember sitting in the waiting room and there was a dad, a kid and a grandad waiting there on the seat in front. I had my head on the chair in front because it was pounding so bad and the kid was saying, 'I'm starving, Dad? Can I have something to eat?' The dad went over to the vending machine and said he'd seen something that cost £2.50. The grandad piped up and said, 'Fucking two 50? Fuck me. Give him two 50, the lad's fucking hungry,' and I was thinking, 'Please don't let this be the last thing I ever hear in this world.'

All of a sudden, a porter and a doctor turned up with a trolley and asked if I could get on. I just about managed to, and they whisked me into a room where there was a woman doctor with long dark hair. She was examining my eyes continually, her hair was brushing my face, and I remember she smelled great and, again, I thought that if this was the end, it wasn't a bad way to go!

Another doctor came in and he said that I hadn't had a brain haemorrhage – but the nurse insisted that I had. He was pulling rank, saying he was the senior doctor and this and that and then she just snapped at him to get whatever it was she was asking for to help me. I had this big blue coat on – the scruffiest coat you've ever seen – and she got some scissors and I said, 'Don't cut that off, love.'

She did though, and she cut my sweatshirt off up to my shoulder as well. Next, it was bang, bang with two syringes and with that she told me I should start to feel better.

I didn't know if I wanted to feel better. I'd had enough and felt I just wanted to go, but after a few minutes the confusion started to pass, and I became a bit more lucid. She wheeled me down for a CT scan and confirmed I had indeed suffered a brain haemorrhage. I was put on a ward but didn't get a wink of sleep because I wasn't allowed to lift my head up. On the bed next to me, there was a guy on a ventilator and the noise was driving me mad. It turned out he had tripped down the stairs and broken his neck, at home. In the morning, his family came to see him, and it was horrible to witness because, mentally, he was no different from how he'd been before the accident, but now he was paralysed and was dying.

I lay there wondering what my outcome would be.

Nobody could tell me how bad it had been or what the lasting effects would be, but eventually they figured it was a bleed between the top of my spine and my brain. In many ways I'd been lucky because, often, if you do survive there are serious mental and physical consequences. I was in hospital for three weeks and I wouldn't be allowed home until I could walk into a room with an occupational therapist and demonstrate that I could make a cup of tea and slice of toast.

When they thought I was ready, we gave it a go. I could see everything I needed to do and what I needed to do, but it was like the Andre Previn sketch with Morecambe and Wise – I was doing all the right things, but not necessarily in the right order. I was devastated and was led back to my bed. I asked what happened next and they said I'd need to get to a convalescence home until I recovered fully because they couldn't keep me at Salford much longer.

I said I wanted to go home and that my family would look after me, but they said I couldn't do that. I just wanted to be with my boys, and everything be normal again. I used to take them to school, pick them up, ferry them here, there and everywhere and then take them to my mum and dad's for tea and I wanted it all to be the same as it had been.

I cried my eyes out that day, but they ended by saying they would give me a few more days at Salford and give the tea and toast exercise another go.

A week later, the same woman took me in and I made an absolute pig's ear of it yet again. She just said, 'That's as near as dammit,' and she said I could go home!

But I was far from being where I needed to be, and I wouldn't work again for 11 months. The haemorrhage had hit me harder than maybe it showed at the time and I was struggling in every way imaginable both mentally and physically.

I was suffering from really bad headaches, and I went to see my surgeon for a progress report after three months and I was a long way from being what I'd consider normal.

I was in a waiting room with people who had hands clawed up and in wheelchairs and they had all suffered brain haemorrhages. It was shocking and unnerving to say the least. I went in to see him with Clare, and after a thorough examination and chat, he said, 'You're fine. You've no disabilities nor any speech impediments. You'll be fine.'

I told him that I was staying in bed all day because I just couldn't be bothered doing anything, which was so unlike me, but he said that would pass in time. So not much changed in the next couple of months and I still had these banging headaches. I'd found the only thing that eased the pain was whisky and it was becoming a problem – but it was the only thing that made me feel better at the time and it worked for me, but it wasn't right and certainly wasn't sustainable.

It had been going on for seven or eight months and I'd had enough, so I called Richard Jobson up at the PFA and explained what had happened and that I needed to see a specialist of some sort. He was shocked when he heard what had happened to me, but he agreed I needed the PFA's help. He arranged an appointment for me to see another specialist – a Mr Cooper – and he would work wonders for me.

It had been 11 months and two weeks since I last worked, but I started dropping the lads off at school again and picking them up, which was hard going because I was absolutely exhausted when I got home. It was around that time that Paul Lake called me to see if I could do something for him on a radio programme he was working on as someone had pulled out.

I said, 'I can't, Lakey. I've had a brain haemorrhage and I'm struggling like mad.' He just said, 'OK mate, no worries, bye.'

I thought when I hung up, 'What was all that about?!' – he hadn't asked me how I was or anything. That wasn't the Lakey I knew and I couldn't figure out why he wasn't that bothered. I should have known better.

Two days later he called and said, 'Mouldy, what did you say you'd had again?' I told him and he said, 'Wow. I thought you'd said something but wasn't sure what it was. How do you feel?'

Lakey was the first person to sit down and talk to me over the phone and ask me how I was, almost a year on from when it first happened. He had a physiotherapy practice and asked me if I could get over to Alderley Edge. We talked about the after-effects I was now living with, and he described the exact same feelings I was having and told me what I needed was a deep-tissue massage.

I went to see him, he got to work on my back and neck, and after he'd finished it was the first time I started to feel genuinely better after almost a year of feeling like death warmed up.

Meanwhile, my mum and dad told me that now I was getting better, I needed to either get back to work or sell the shop because they couldn't do it anymore. Mum was just telling me straight, and as harsh as it seemed, she was telling me what I needed to hear, so I phased myself back to work, but it was utterly exhausting to begin with. At first, I couldn't count how many chicken nuggets were in the fryer and the headaches continued, so there was still an element of confusion and occasional issues with seemingly the simplest of tasks.

Mr Cooper, the surgeon, advised me on things I should avoid and explained why I needed to change my routine. He also pointed out to me that this was not going to be a quick recovery. He explained that it could be five years before I got back to anything like I was prior to the bleed.

Given my history of injuries and the recovery time, I was sure that for me it wouldn't take so long. How wrong I was! Mr Cooper was an expert in his field, and he was bang on.

Eventually, though, the headaches did become less frequent and, as I write this in 2022, they have stopped altogether. I'm told I've made a decent recovery. Clare and I split about five years back – it was just one of those things and, while she'll always be the mother of my lads, we were better off going our separate ways. After the brain haemorrhage, I was a different person with different values and parting ways was the right thing to do.

Michelle Lake – no relation to Paul – and I got together after my divorce; I don't know what I'd have done without her help and support through two of the biggest events in my life.

After almost 25 years, I finally sold my chippy in 2021, after deciding to take things a bit easier. I wanted to focus on my lads more and just lead a bit of a more relaxed life.

As for the boys, they're all doing well in their own way.

Joe is in the USA now. Like me, he started at Bolton Lads, but then he went to Manchester United. Sadly, he had a hip impingement, aged 15, a big problem to have as a youngster, and they released him at 16. He then went to Blackpool and did well while Owen Oyston was in charge, but they had managers coming in and out like nobody's business and he was released. After that, he decided he was better than what he was being offered here in England.

A friend we knew encouraged Joe to consider a scholarship in the US. He took the advice and went to Indianapolis where he achieved a degree at Butler University. It was there that he met a true gent in his coach Paul Snape. Joe, unfortunately, had to retire from playing because the pain in his hip was driving him to distraction.

Joe is now married to Brianna, who he met at Butler, and they now live together in South Georgia where he is studying for his master's and is moving into coaching at South Georgia University.

Ted started at Bolton Lads as well, then went to Blackburn Rovers and on to Blackpool. With what had happened to Joe, I was hyper-aware of kids being led down paths of disappointment, and I could see it could happen with Ted as they weren't willing to give him any guarantees about the future.

At Blackpool, Ted was the player of the year aged 14. I went to the parents' evening the following week and because of what had happened to Joe, I asked for a pro contract for Ted. They weren't prepared to offer him one, so I asked for him to be released. I told Blackpool there was no other option, and eventually they released him as, really, they had no choice in the matter. Ted hurt his ankle but went for a trial at Bolton and academy manager Jimmy Phillips saw that he had the running power of an attacking full-back, so he switched him from midfield to full-back. I had to bite my tongue but I was wrong, and he flourished there.

Ted scored eight goals in his first season as a scholar from full-back, but then he hurt his ankle coming down from an innocuous aerial challenge and I knew he'd done something serious straight away. To cut a long story short, the club sent him to see a specialist who told him he had to retire because one side of his ankle was lopsided. It was a one in 200 million chance – they said that the condition he had was that rare. Unconvinced and desperate to get him right, we went seeing specialist after specialist, looking for a better prognosis, but the outcome was the same; they all said his ankle would only get worse. I couldn't believe there was nothing they could do for him, but I was told by one expert that he'd just been 'dealt a really bad hand'. Bolton looked after him, though, and kept him involved, and today he's got the kit manager's job and that has kept a smile on his face.

Louie started at Liverpool before moving on to Manchester City and one day he called me up to say he'd broken his wrist, and I thought, 'Here we go again.' He then tore his cartilage and then he broke his other wrist – all in his three years with City.

He moved to Wolves in 2021 and has spent much of that first season on loan at Ebbsfleet. He played nearly 30 games in total in 2021/22, which was good for him. He needs to just keep his head down, work hard and, hopefully, he'll get the right kind of breaks and make a good career for himself.

Today, like my dad and grandad used to do with me, I go and watch Louie whenever and wherever he plays, just like I've done with all three of my lads. Ted lives with me in Bolton and I go over to the States to see Joe whenever I can. I see my mum and dad regularly as they only live around the corner from me, and I'm enjoying retirement while keeping busy.

So, that's about it.

My ghostwriter decided the title with the 'extraordinary' angle down to my goals as a kid and extraordinary bad luck with injuries.

After almost 55 years on this planet, the big question is – what have I learned so far in life? First, appreciate every day and don't take your loved ones for granted because you can never predict what's around the corner.

If I had to describe my life to date, I'd say it's been exciting, hard work, sometimes disappointing, definitely memorable and I wouldn't change any of it.

What part of my life have I most enjoyed?

Well, I've had two lives really – one scoring goals and the other frying chips. I'd like to think I was pretty good at both those things.

Backwords

AS AN alternative to forewords, some people wished to contribute with their own tributes to Paul and his career. 'Backwords' might be a little unusual, but they're well worth including.

Brent Peters

Owner and manager, Bacup Borough

Having good connections throughout football and the north-west in particular, I was well aware of Paul Moulden's reputation as a natural goalscorer long before I first met him.

I was director of football for Accrington Stanley in June 1996 and the manager at the time was a guy called Stan Allen.

I learned Paul was unattached but had also heard that he was a bit disillusioned with football and concentrating more on his chip-shop business.

I got in touch with him and managed to convince him to come and play for us, hopefully getting his appetite back in the process. It wasn't easy, but I managed to get the deal over the line, and I couldn't have been happier.

Eric Whalley was the chairman back then, and I recall Stan Allen was ill for the first few games of the 1996/97 season and his assistant took on first-team duties in his absence.

For whatever reason, he didn't pick Paul for the starting XI away to Colwyn Bay and Eric Whalley went ballistic as he was something of a coup for the club. Stan Allen lost his job not that long after Paul arrived, and Tony Greenwood came in, but he wanted to bring his own players in and Paul decided he'd seen enough and packed it in.

I went on to work for Doncaster Rovers, Bury and Rotherham United but I was between jobs when Bacup Borough came along to see if I could give them a hand as they were struggling at the time, and I lived nearby. I told them I'd help out for a bit, but I would be moving on at some stage as I wanted to get back into league football.

That was 25 years ago! I ended up buying the club and becoming manager, coach, owner and chairman!

One of my first tasks was to tempt Paul to come out of retirement – he was still only 30 or so – which I managed to do, and he came to play for me.

He made his debut in December 1997 and scored in a 2-2 draw – which didn't surprise me! He enjoyed his time with us and for the 1998/99 season I made him captain and brought in his old City team-mate Darren Beckford – so we had two former City strikers up front, which caught the media's attention.

Paul stayed at Bacup for four years and was a true professional throughout. In the end, I think he was concerned that if he picked up a major injury, he'd struggle with work, and so had to prioritise his business over football, but he scored goals for us and was never less than a top lad during his time with us.

I can't speak highly enough of Paul Moulden, and it was a genuine pleasure having him in my team. I admired him for many years, and everyone connected with youth football knew what he was capable of as a kid and in his early career. He was some talent.

You won't find many players who were unluckier with injuries during their career, and an injury-free Paul Moulden would have played at the very top level – and I don't mean just in this country, I'm talking Europe as well. He'd have been up here with some of the best strikers. There is no doubt in my mind about that, and I don't say that lightly either, but the game was cruel to him.

He epitomised what being a true professional was all about and yet I never once heard him complain about the bad luck he'd suffered, which says everything about him as a man.

Brent Peters, Bacup, July 2022

* * *

Julian Darby
Former Bolton Lads, Bolton Wanderers and Coventry City player

I think I first started playing in the same Bolton Lads side as Paul when we were around ten. Prior to that, I'd played against him at primary school level when he was at St Osmond's, and I was at Park Road Bolton School.

It was a semi-final at a school in Breightmet and I remember that clearly as it was one of the few occasions he didn't score as we won 1-0! With most players, a particular goal or incident was why you remembered them, but with Paul it was the games he didn't score that stuck out. You remembered them because they were as rare as hen's teeth!

We'd both heard of each other and there was a mutual respect between us.

Our first year at Bolton Lads Club was disappointing because we actually drew a game – the rest we won. It was a great group of youngsters and we just won almost every game we played.

I couldn't tell you how many goals I scored because I never kept count, and I didn't know how many Paul scored until the news came out that he'd set a new world record. I probably managed about half the amount he got, which I suppose is pretty decent in itself.

He was an instinctive finisher who was strong and powerful. He could run all day – and I mean all day. I remember at a Bolton Schools cross-country competition, you always had a hare being dragged out front showing you which way to go, and he was out at the front (as usual) shouting that the hare needed to speed up! He was incredibly fit.

I'd actually forgotten how many goals he scored for Bolton Lads, so to see some of his stats – 16 goals in one game – my word, it took some doing. He always shared the credit and thanked his team-mates, and it was never all about Paul with Paul. He had no ego in that respect.

I coach at Bolton Wanderers' academy these days and I remember saying to the lads at one session, 'Come on, we need a bit of telepathy here.' I wanted my number nine and number ten to play instinctively and know what each other would do and be on the same wavelength.

I think Paul and I found that wavelength, because I always knew what he was going to do, which made my job a little bit easier. Once he was in behind, it was invariably a goal because he very rarely missed the target. He could score any type of goal. From a distance, from an angle, tap-ins, headers, one on ones, volleys; you name it, he could do it all with either foot. I can't ever recall him chipping anyone, but as he ended up with his own chippy, I guess he more than made up for that after his career.

At Bolton Lads, we were winning games by big margins and whenever we had the bigger games, cup semi-finals or finals, we could always raise our games to another level.

We were a tight-knit group who had each other's backs and, looking back, it was a special time. I was lucky enough to go on and have a good professional career with Bolton Wanderers, Coventry and West Brom (among others) and Paul made it into City's first team before moving on to find regular first-team football elsewhere. Injuries hurt him and held him back, there is no doubt about that.

Paul thinks he might have played against me professionally on one occasion when he was at Brighton on loan and I was playing for Wanderers, but I can't recall that game for some reason.

Paul was one of the most gifted strikers I ever came across in my career and I enjoyed every minute I played alongside him. He was an athlete with extraordinary finishing ability, and he had strength, pace and power. Clubs were queuing up to sign him and, if he was around today, you can only guess at the scramble to sign him there would be.

There weren't many strikers capable of banging 16 goals in one game around then, and there isn't today.

He was a one-off.

Julian Darby, Bolton May 2022

* * *

Tony Book
Former Manchester City captain and manager

I first heard of Paul Moulden through our scouting network and the information I had was something along the lines of 'we need to sign this kid'.

He was banging goals in for Bolton Lads and just about every top club in the country were after him, but we had one advantage – he was a Manchester City fan.

He came from a good, knowledgeable football family and we invited him to train with us. I knew he'd been training with Everton, United, Leeds and several other clubs, but after watching him in a trial match, I quickly understood we had to bring him to City and were willing to match any offers for his services.

I was the City youth-team coach at the time along with Glyn Pardoe and we were assembling quite a group of talented young players. You could tell Paul was very much at ease with being at City and once we'd spelled out how we saw his future with us would be, he signed a two-year YTS deal.

The only thing Paul had going against him was his physique – he'd grown quickly as a boy and stood out at schoolboy level, but now he was among other lads his age who had caught him up, he looked fairly light to be a traditional number nine.

But of course, that didn't stop him.

His fitness was superb, and he was razor-sharp in or around the box. The boy was a natural goalscorer and I know some of the lads thought he was my favourite – and they were right!

I loved his outlook, and he was a great lad to have in the dressing room.

He always worked his socks off, had an infectious, positive attitude and was great for the squad.

We had a wonderful youth team and, in 1986, we won the FA Youth Cup – and it was Paul's goals that made the difference on our way to beating United over two legs in the final.

The lad was so unlucky with major injuries during his younger years, and they sort of caught up with him later on. But for them, I am certain he would have gone all the way to the top.

He was the most talented natural goalscorer I came across in my career as a player, manager or coach. He was that good.

It was a pleasure having him in my side and I will always wonder how far he might have gone but for those injury issues.

But he still had a good, solid career that he should be proud of.

Tony Book, Sale, March 2022

* * *

Fred Eyre

Former Manchester City player and best-selling author

I knew about Paul Moulden first and foremost because I knew his dad Tony really well. When I was a kid at City, all the junior teams played in the various divisions of the Lancashire League, as was the way in those days.

Tony played for Blackburn Rovers, and I played against him on a few occasions because he was always my direct opponent. He was two years older than me and a bit more mature – and he never ever shut up for the whole 90 minutes!

Then he popped up at Bury and it was a case of, 'My God, where's my earplugs?' He later played for Rochdale and Peterborough United – where he played alongside Derek Dougan – and later again for Notts County.

The ages we played at would be when I was 17, 18 and 19 and he was 19, 20 and 21. Tony had enjoyed a decent career and lived in Bolton, and we'd bump into each other every now and then and catch up.

Finally, when we were both bollocksed physically, we ended up at Radcliffe Borough towards the end of our careers and, finally, we were team-mates. Instead of getting under my skin with his constant yapping, he was now alongside me yapping at the opposition – which was a blessing – and we played together for several years.

We'd both seen better days, but we played because we enjoyed it and wanted to carry on playing for as long as we could. One thing you always got from Tony was maximum effort, no matter what. He gave all he could give for the full 90 minutes, and I think he instilled that in Paul.

Tony's dad, Joe, and his son, Paul, were a close footballing family who were like clones of one another! They all looked the spit of each other and when Paul started his exploits, Tony and Joe would always be there watching him and guiding him.

Word soon spread of Paul's goalscoring achievements for Bolton Lads, and it was common knowledge that he was banging in an average of something like five per game – sometimes double figures – and you couldn't be a football person in the area and not know of a kid who was doing that. Even more so in my case because I knew his dad and grandad, so I maybe took more interest in his career because of that.

The truth was, he was just too good for his age group. Paul was not a big beast who knocked people around, he was just too good for the levels he played at in his younger years. That levels itself out over the time, but back then he scored at will. He knew nothing else, and he just wanted to score as many goals as he could every time he played.

I knew he was a special talent from the games I saw him play in for Bolton Lads. I used to go along to some matches with Stuart White, David White's dad, especially when they were both signed up by City, and I could have taken my grandmother along and she would have said, 'Who's the number nine?'

Anyone who went and watched one of the games that he was playing couldn't fail to be impressed by what he was doing and that he was the best player.

I'd played with lads of a similar stature when I was a junior, but none who scored as many goals as Paul did. Ray Hewitt was a contemporary of mine for Manchester Schoolboys and you just knew they would go on to achieve something in the game. But I also saw boys who were as strong as Paul was at his age but didn't progress when other lads caught them up physically.

He wasn't the same as his dad, but he reminded me of him because of certain mannerisms and characteristics. He was single-minded and you could tell he'd been brought up like Alan Ball, with a dad on the touchline, always pushing him, encouraging him and shouting advice. Football was in his blood.

I'd see Tony talking to him immediately after the game, saying stuff like, 'You played well and, OK, you scored eight, but don't forget you missed two so let's work on that.' He kept his feet on the ground. Paul was driven by the will of his dad and every time he played, he was determined to get in as many shots as possible. If you shoot and get it on target, you always have a chance of scoring.

I would have defied anyone to have watched him play for Bolton Lads and not think he was going to go on and have a good career as a professional footballer. And he did.

At City, he was still head and shoulders above his team-mates in the youth team. But three broken legs will inevitably take a little bit of pace away from you and I'm not sure Paul had that extra pace to lose to begin with.

Some players are so fast that they can lose a yard of speed through injury and still be quicker than most others when they recover, but Paul just didn't have any slack to play with and so, as he returned from a major setback, he was a little slower each time, which is nothing more than bad luck. It eventually took its toll on his body and his career and it all became a little more like hard work rather than all the natural ability he had as a teenager.

Fred Eyre, Manchester, May 2022